1 MONTH OF
FREE
READING

at

www.ForgottenBooks.com

By purchasing this book you are eligible for one month membership to ForgottenBooks.com, giving you unlimited access to our entire collection of over 1,000,000 titles via our web site and mobile apps.

To claim your free month visit:

www.forgottenbooks.com/free922027

ISBN 978-0-260-01057-5
PIBN 10922027

Vol. 2, No. 4      April, 1915

DOMINION OF CANADA

DEPARTMENT OF AGRICULTURE

The Agricultural Gazette

of Canada

EDITOR: J. B. SPENCER, B.S.A.

Issued by direction of

THE HONOURABLE MARTIN BURRELL

Minister of Agriculture

OTTAWA

GOVERNMENT PRINTING BUREAU

1915

CONTENTS.

	PAGE
The Potato	307
Agricultural Conferences	308
The System of Publicity	311

PART I.

DOMINION DEPARTMENT OF AGRICULTURE.

The Dominion Experimental Farms:—

The Division of Horticulture:

Growing Potatoes for Home and Market, by W. T. Macoun, Dominion Horticulturist ... 319

The Division of Botany:

The Control of Potato Diseases, by H. T. Güssow, Dominion Botanist ... 323

Education as an Aid in the Control of Plant Diseases, by W. A. McCubbin, Plant Pathologist ... 325

The Division of Apiculture:

The Bee Keeping Situation in Canada, by F. W. L. Sladen, Apiarist, Experimental Farms System ... 325

The Fruit Branch:—

Marketing the Peach Crop, by C. W. Baxter, Chief Fruit Inspector for Eastern Ontario ... 328

Notes ... 329

The Entomological Branch:

The Control of Cutworms, by Arthur Gibson, Chief Assistant Entomologist ... 330

The Health of Animals Branch:—

Tuberculosis in Swine, by F. Torrance, Veterinary Director General ... 332

PART II.

PROVINCIAL DEPARTMENTS OF AGRICULTURE.

Potato Growing:—

Prince Edward Island, by Theodore Ross, Secretary for Agriculture ... 334

Nova Scotia, by F. L. Fuller, Superintendent of Agricultural Societies ... 335

New Brunswick, by J. B. Daggett, Secretary for Agriculture ... 338

Quebec, by the Rev. H. Bois, Professor of Agronomy ... 339

Macdonald College, by T. G. Bunting, Professor of Horticulture ... 340

Ontario, by Prof. C. A. Zavitz, Ontario Agricultural College ... 342

Manitoba, by S. A. Bedford, Deputy Minister of Agriculture ... 348

Saskatchewan, by J. Bracken, Professor of Field Husbandry ... 350

Alberta, by Geo. Harcourt, Deputy Minister of Agriculture ... 351

British Columbia, by W. Newton, Assistant Soil and Crop Inspector ... 353

Quebec:—

Agricultural Legislation ... 356

Maple Sugar Industry, by J. Antonio Grenier, Secretary for Agriculture ... 357

Ontario:—

Demonstration Lectures for Women's Institutes, by Geo. A. Putnam, Ontario Department of Agriculture ... 358

PART III.

PROVINCIAL DEPARTMENTS OF EDUCATION.

Domestic Science in the Schools:—   PAGE

Nova Scotia, by A. H. Mackay, Superintendent of Education................. 362

New Brunswick, by Fletcher Peacock, Director of Manual Training and Domestic Science.. 363

Quebec, by Rev. O. E. Martin, Agricultural School of Ste. Anne de la Pocatiere. 364

Ontario, compiled from official publications......................... 365

Manitoba, by R. Fletcher, Deputy Minister of Education.................... 367

Saskatchewan, by D. P. McColl.. 367

Alberta, by Charles C. Miller, Director of Technical Education.............. 368

British Columbia, by Alexander Robinson, Superintendent of Education........ 369

Relationship of the School Garden to the Class Room:—

Nova Scotia, by L. A. DeWolfe, Director Rural Science Schools.............. 371

New Brunswick, by R. P. Steeves, Director Elementary Agricultural Education. 372

Manitoba, by H. W. Watson, Director Elementary Agricultural Education..... 374

British Columbia, by J. W. Gibson, Director Elementary Agricultural Education... 375

Teaching Agriculture in the Rural Schools of Quebec, by Jean Charles Magnan, B.S.A., District Representative... 376

Preparation and Mounting of Weeds for Class and Reference Work, by Faith Fyles, Assistant Botanist, Central Experimental Farm........................... 377

PART IV.

SPECIAL CONTRIBUTIONS, REPORTS OF AGRICULTURAL ORGANIZATIONS, NOTES AND PUBLICATIONS

The Work of the Canadian Seed Growers' Association with Potato Crop, by L. H. Newman, Secretary, Ottawa.. 381

Potato Growing Contest in Manitoba.................................... 385

Production of Potatoes.. 386

Cultivation on Vacant Lots. A Practical Demonstration from Philadelphia........ 387

Milking Regulations... 389

Financial Assistance to Agriculture..................................... 390

Co-operative Experiments in Weed Eradication........................... 391

Classes for the Study of Birds.. 392

Co-operative Wool Marketing in Saskatchewan............................ 392

Home Economics in Manitoba... 393

Agriculture in Rural Schools... 393

County Agent Earns $410,000.. 393

College Extension Work... 394

Societies and Associations:—

Prince Edward Island Poultry Association............................ 395

New Brunswick Farmers' and Dairymen's Association.................. 395

Saskatchewan Veterinary Association................................ 395

British Columbia Fruit Growers' Association......................... 396

Junior Farmers' Improvement Association............................ 396

Good Roads Association... 396

Cattle Breeders' Association of Manitoba............................ 396

North Battleford Live Stock Company................................ 397

Live Stock Associations of Saskatchewan............................ 397

Book Reviews.. 398

New Publications.. 399

The Dominion Department of Agriculture............................. 399

The Provincial Departments of Agriculture........................... 400

Miscellaneous... 401

Notes.. 401

Index to Periodical Literature.. 403

The Agricultural Gazette
OF CANADA

VOL. II   APRIL, 1915   No. 4

THE AGRICULTURAL GAZETTE of Canada is published monthly, in English and in French, by the Dominion Department of Agriculture. It is not intended for general circulation. A limited number of copies, however, are available to subscribers at $1.00 per annum, or 10 cents per copy.

Subscriptions should be forwarded to the Editor, Agricultural Gazette, Ottawa.

THE POTATO

ALTHOUGH it is recorded that the potato (*Solanum tuberosum*) was used as human food more than a thousand years ago, its culture did not extend beyond the boundaries of South America until about the middle of the sixteenth century. To Sir Walter Raleigh is credited the introduction of the potato into England and in 1586 it was definitely known to have been grown in Ireland. Since that time the cultivation of this crop has extended over the civilized globe. So great has the reliance upon it become that when blight occurred in Europe at various times during the past three-quarters of a century, the failure of the crop was attended by serious famine conditions.

The potato has acquired a position next to wheat, for human consumption, in the annual field crops of the world and enormous quantities are utilized in the arts and for stock food. The world's crop of potatoes exceeds that of wheat by some two billion bushels. Valuing wheat at one dollar and potatoes at fifty cents per bushel, the world's crop in 1912 may be set down at an approximate worth of $3,800,000,000 for wheat and $3,000,000,000 for potatoes. Last year the figures for Canada were, for wheat 161,280,000 bushels, valued at $196,418,000, and for potatoes 85,672,000 bushels, valued at $41,598,000.

Last year was a good year for potatoes, as a yield of 180 bushels per acre was harvested over Canada, which was some twenty bushels higher than the average for the past five seasons. Even the yield of 1914 leaves a wide margin before the reasonably full crop is reached, as from 400 to 450 bushels per acre are commonly grown where the recognized conditions for success are applied to the soil, the seed and the growing crop. The improvement in the potato in fruitfulness, quality and freedom from disease has engaged the energies of experts in many parts of Canada. The outstanding features of what is being done and the lessons learned by the Dominion and Provincial Departments of Agriculture, the Canadian Seed Growers' Association and Macdonald College, are brought together in this issue of THE AGRICULTURAL GAZETTE.

AGRICULTURAL CONFERENCES

THE Agricultural Conferences among farmers in each section of the different provinces arranged by the Dominion Department of Agriculture, as a part of the campaign to encourage increased production by improved methods of farming, and to distribute detailed and complete information as to the needs of the Empire, and the opportunities available owing to changed conditions of production throughout the world, have been completed in all the provinces excepting Quebec, where a second series, owing to the success of the first, has been thought desirable. The Department has been represented at each of the conferences by a committee of three. Two of the delegation discussed practical agriculture, while the other representative delivered an address of a patriotic character. The various provinces were organized in different ways, there being one officer in each province to supervise the work. His duty was to select the places of meetings; to advertise the conferences and arrange for local speakers and presiding officers. Approximately 554 conferences have been held, divided as follows among the different provinces:

Prince Edward Island, 43; Nova Scotia, 30; New Brunswick, 40; Quebec, 210; Ontario, 101; Manitoba, 25; Saskatchewan, 46; Alberta, 44; British Columbia, 28.

The conferences were arranged for different dates in different provinces. The first conference was held in Prince Edward Island on January 5th, and the last conferences, except in Quebec, as previously mentioned, were held in Northern Ontario and Saskatchewan on April 3rd.

In Prince Edward Island, where a large number of Conferences were held in small places and close together, the average attendance was about 130.

In Nova Scotia the meetings have been wonderfully successful in general, and some additional conferences were arranged to comply with local requests.

In New Brunswick conferences were held in both the French and English districts. A large portion of the potato crop of 1914 was left in the hands of the producers on account of the lack of ocean transport facilities. The suggestion was made that more oats and more hay should be grown, and in the wheat-growing sections more efforts should be made to produce a home supply of breadstuffs. It is thought that the campaign will help to increase the grain area very considerably. Several additional conferences were requested and arranged for.

In the Eastern Townships in Quebec, the average attendance at twenty-four meetings was 175. In some sections the subjects taken up were, principally, the better selection of seed grains; treatment for smut; better cultivation; growing of more silage and roots, to make more economical food for stock; advising the saving of all the best breeding animals so as to increase the food supply. The one point which was emphasized very strongly was the keeping of more sheep, especially in this section, on account of the rough pastures which are getting very much infested with noxious weeds; and on account of the prospect of wool being high, the value of sheep as meat production, and the very little labour required in connection with the care of same.

In the French speaking districts of Quebec, the conferences were arranged by the Live Stock Branch of the Department and at 114 meetings,

PATRIOTISM and PRODUCTION

The Call of the Empire to the Farmers of Canada

"Approximately twenty million men have been mobilized in Europe. A large proportion of these have been withdrawn from the farms of the countries at war. Even in neutral countries large numbers of food producers have been called from the land to be ready for emergencies. It is difficult for us to realize what will be the effect on food production through the withdrawal of several million men from all the great agricultural countries of Europe. These millions cease to be producers, they have become consumers,—worse still, they have become destroyers of food."

HON. MARTIN BURRELL, Minister of Agriculture.

Britain must have food—food this year, and food next year. Britain is looking to Canada to supply most of that food. We are sending our surplus now, but we must prepare for a larger surplus this year and next year. Patriotism and Production must go hand in hand.

Because of this need of the Empire for more food, and the call to Canada in that need, the Canadian Department of Agriculture has arranged for a series of Conferences throughout the Dominion, with the object of giving suggestions as to the best ways of increasing production of the particular products needed at this time.

ATTEND YOUR CONFERENCE

At these Conferences agricultural specialists, who have studied agricultural conditions and production throughout the world, and the best means of increasing agricultural production in Canada, will give valuable information and suggestions to the farmers, live-stock men, dairymen, poultrymen, vegetable growers, and other producers of this country. The Canadian Department of Agriculture urges you to attend as many of these Conferences as possible; also to watch for other information on the subject that will be given in other announcements in this newspaper.

Put Energy into Production of Staple Foods

The Government does not ask farmers to work harder, so much as it urges them to make their work more productive, and to produce those staple foods that the Empire most needs and that can be most easily stored and transported

Europe, and particularly Britain, will need the following staple foods from Canada more than ever before:

Wheat, oats, corn, beans, peas.

Beef, mutton, bacon, and ham.

Cheese and butter.

Poultry and eggs.

Vegetables, such as potatoes, onions, and turnips.

The larger the yield of these staple food products, the greater the service to the Empire. Germany in the last ten years has doubled the average yield of the majority of her field crops largely through better seed, thorough cultivation and use of fertilizer. But in making your plans, don't let your enthusiasm and loyalty make you attempt more than you can carry through. Millions of bushels, instead of millions of acres, should be the aim of Canadian farmers. And while the Empire's armies are busy putting down German Militarism, let us at home appropriate the best of Germany's agricultural methods for the Empire's advantage.

The Government urges farmers, stockmen, dairymen and other producers to make a wider use of the Free Bulletins issued by the Canadian Department of Agriculture.

This Department has issued over two hundred bulletins. A list of bulletins is printed in a booklet entitled "Publications Available for Distribution."

Clip out, fill in and mail the coupon below and get this booklet. Then select the bulletins that will be of value to you. Mail your coupon right now. Address the envelope to Publications Branch, Canadian Department of Agriculture, Ottawa. Do not put a stamp on the envelope. No stamp is necessary. Your coupon will be "On His Majesty's Service."

Give expression to your desire to assist the Empire in this crisis by co-operating in this great "Patriotism and Production" movement.

Canadian Department of Agriculture, Ottawa, Canada

Publications Branch, Canadian Department of Agriculture, Ottawa.

Please send list of Publications Available for Distribution.

Name..

P.O. Address..

County .... Prov...................

included in the first series, the attendance averaged at least 200. It is reported that in certain districts the numbers present ranged from 300 to 800 people. It is stated, on good authority, that these were the most successful agricultural conferences ever held in the province, the numbers of people present being 60 per cent in excess of the average attendance at rural conferences on other occasions. The interest on the part of the farmers was very keen and evidently represented a desire on their part to meet the situation which was presented to them in an earnest and patriotic way. Large numbers of ladies were present at each meeting. The success of the campaign may be attributed, in no small degree, to the co-operation of the clergy of all denominations and particularly of the priests of the various parishes. The publicity given the work in Quebec has been due very largely to their efforts and, through their attendance at the meetings and the appropriate addresses which they delivered, the movement for increased production in the province received a very strong impetus.

In Ontario the average attendance at each conference was 186. The reports received show that the importance of conserving the good breeding stock is realized and that it is recognized that while farm labour is a serious problem, production can be increased with little additional work by seed selection, and the use of good varieties. One of the reports states: "Farmers well realize the part they have to bear in the present war. Great feeling of patriotism shown, Willing to economize that more foodstuffs might be offered. Selection of varieties and cultivation paramount factors." At the large centres considerable interest was aroused in the question of making use of vacant lots and backyards for vegetable gardens.

A report from Manitoba states: "Most of the meetings held to date have been excellent in every way; in many cases the farmers have expressed themselves to the extent of saying that the conference was the best farmers' meeting ever held in the district."

In Saskatchewan the attendance is reported as an average of 60 in small towns, and 400 in larger places.

Alberta—The attendance at meetings varies from 50 to 250. The meetings here were completed on March 22nd. A keen interest was taken in the discussions, and there was a desire to take advantage of all the information which could be secured.

The returns indicate that the conferences were attended by some of the best class of farmers, who showed an anxiety to do what they could to assist the Empire and a desire to discuss with others the best plan by which under present conditions the production of food supplies could be increased. There is great unanimity in the reports, showing the general impression that production can and would be increased by certain well-recognized principles: (1) Seed selection; (2) thorough cultivation; (3) proper fertilization.

In addition, however, one of the chief objects in holding these conferences was to gather information as to difficulties met with by the farmer in increasing agricultural production, and there are three things which suggest themselves in the official reports already received, viz.:—

The difficulty of securing efficient farm help; the necessity of some system to provide agricultural credits; the need of an organized system of marketing agricultural products.

THE SYSTEM OF PUBLICITY

TO direct attention to the conferences, and to emphasize the work they were instituted to perform, a unique system and style of advertising was adopted. Not alone did this advertising attract much attention on its own account, but it has been the subject of considerable eulogium from a variety of sources. Its originality of method and its effectiveness of character, it will be observed, have been thought worthy of preservation in the pages of THE GAZETTE. There were inserted in daily and weekly newspapers covering the country from coast to coast, a series of nine boldly displayed and appropriately worded advertisements, fac-similes of all of which are produced. Each, it will be noticed, makes a specialty of some branch, this one, for instance, of staple foods, that of the farm labour problem, the next of fertilization and cultivation, the fourth of live stock, the fifth of the variety of foods required, the sixth of the splendid work women can do, the seventh of the need of greater poultry production, the eighth of the service that vegetable growers can render, and the ninth of the good use cities and towns could make of waste lands and vacant lots. All struck the one note, namely, that whatever is done should be done well. It was pointed out again and again at the conferences that it was neither increased acreage nor harder work that was asked of the farmer, but the greatest care in the preparation of the soil on the one hand, and earnest attention, on the other, to the selection of pure seed and the choice of breeding stock. That this meant both improved and increased production was the truth and impression it was sought to convey.

Evidence of the success of the advertising is furnished in a result that cannot be disputed. In the right hand corner of each display was printed a coupon inviting application for bulletins, pamphlets, records and reports issued by The Publications Branch of the Department of Agriculture at Ottawa. So great has been the demand that not only have several editions been exhausted, but in other cases the quantity asked for individually was so large that correspondence resulted which involved delay. While the utmost regret is felt that it has been found impossible to respond promptly to every application, it is also felt that the vigour with which the campaign had to be conducted placed the foretelling of the overwhelming demand out of the question.

PATRIOTISM and PRODUCTION

Complete Now Your Plans for the Year's Work

Canada, this year, cannot produce too much staple food. No matter how large her surplus for export, there will still be need of more food in Europe and Britain. The Canadian Government, therefore, urges all farmers and producers of food to attend the series of Conferences now being held throughout the Dominion under the direction of the Canadian Department of Agriculture. Let farmers get together at these Conferences and discuss the vital questions of the day. Agricultural Specialists will also be on hand to give valuable information as to the food products the Empire and her Allies most need, and to offer suggestions to increase production.

ATTEND YOUR CONFERENCE

The important thing now is, to complete at once your plan for the year's work — for increased production. By planning well in advance, each month's operations can be carried through more effectively when the time comes. Delays later on, through neglect of this, will mean loss to you and to the Empire.

Use the Best Seed

This year, for the sake of the Empire, farmers should be exceptionally careful in the selection of seed. Cheap seed is often the dearest. If every Canadian farmer would use only the best varieties, and sow on properly cultivated soil, the grain output of Canadian farms would be doubled. Deal only with reliable seedsmen. Write at once to Canadian Department of Agriculture, Ottawa, and to your Provincial Agricultural Department, for information as to the best varieties of seed to be used in your particular locality, and use no others.

All grain intended for seed should be thoroughly cleaned and selected to retain only the strong kernels. You can reap only what you sow. It does not pay to sow weeds. Clean seed means larger crops and helps to keep the land clean. When you have your seed grain ready, put it through the cleaner once more.

Test Your Seed

Test your seed for vitality, too. Seed is not always as good as it looks. For example, oats, quite normal in appearance and weight, may be so badly damaged by frost that their value for seed is completely destroyed. If you have any doubt as to the quality of your seed a sample may be sent free to the seed laboratory at Ottawa, or Calgary, for test. But, in most cases this simple test will prove sufficient:—

Take a saucer and two pieces of blotting paper. Place seed between blotting papers. Keep moist and in a warm place. In a few days, you will be able to see whether the vitality is there. Neglect to test your seed may mean the loss of crop.

The Farm Labour Problem

This is undoubtedly one of the most difficult problems to solve today. There is a surplus of labour in the cities and towns and a shortage in the country. Careful handling of the problem is necessary. Under present conditions, in addition to looking to the Governments for help, the necessary work should be largely undertaken locally.

Committees in every Town

The Government suggests the forming of an active committee in every town and city, composed of town and country men and women. This committee would find out the sort of help the farmers of their locality need, and get a list of the unemployed in their town or city, who are suitable for farm labour. With this information, the committee would be in a good position to get the right man for the right place.

Councils, both rural and urban, boards of trade and other organizations could advantageously finance such work. Every unemployed man in the town or city who is placed on the farm becomes immediately a producer, instead of a mere consumer and a civic expense. With Britain and her Allies calling for more food, it will be a national loss, in fact a national crime, to leave in the towns and cities any unemployed men who are capable, as thousands of them are, of being of assistance on the farm.

Have you a house on the farm for a married man? A real home for the farm labourer will solve this problem.

Free Bulletins

The Government urges farmers and other producers to make a wider use of the large number of Free Bulletins issued by the Canadian Department of Agriculture, Ottawa, or your Provincial Departments. There are special Bulletins on selection of seed, testing, early planting, that you should have. Clip out, fill in and mail the coupon below and get these Bulletins.

Send your coupon by first mail. Do not put a stamp on the envelope. Your coupon will be "On His Majesty's Service," and will travel free.

Canadian Department of Agriculture, Ottawa, Canada

Publications Branch, Canadian Department of Agriculture, Ottawa.

Please send me Bulletins relating to Seed.

Name ....

P.O. Address ....

County .... Prov. ....

12

PATRIOTISM and PRODUCTION

"Belgium as a producing factor is obliterated from the map. Britain, always unable to sustain itself, will have stronger needs. That beautiful section of France where a little more than a year ago I saw the countless stooks of golden grain is now scarred with the deep-dug trenches. Surely, surely there is need for all that we can do."

HON. MARTIN BURRELL, Minister of Agriculture.

The Empire Needs Many Foods

The Empire asks Canada to increase the production of staple foods—not merely of wheat. Great Britain wants oats, corn, barley, peas, beans, potatoes, turnips, onions, meat, dairy products, poultry and eggs.

In the past Great Britain has imported immense quantities of these staple foods from Russia, France, Belgium, Germany, and Austria-Hungary as shown by the following:

Average Imports
Years 1910-1913

Wheat	28,439,609 bush.
Oats	23,586,304 "
Barley	15,192,268 "
Corn	7,621,374 "
Peas	703,058 "
Beans	639,553 "
Potatoes	4,721,590 "
Onions	271,569 "
Meat	26,509,766 lbs.
Eggs	121,112,916 doz.
Butter and Cheese	91,765,233 lbs.

The above mentioned sources of supply of staple foods are now, in the main, cut off as result of the war. Great Britain is looking to Canada to supply a large share of the shortage. Every individual farmer has a duty to perform.

Make Your Land Produce More

Millions of bushels rather than millions of acres should be Canada's aim. The fields already under cultivation should be made more productive. Keep in good good seed and good cultivation.

That there is abundant reason to expect larger returns from the same area is conclusively shown when we compare the average production of the present time with the possible production. Note the following brief table which shows our average in 1914 and the possible production per acre:—

	Average	Possible
Fall Wheat	20.43	52.
Spring Wheat	14.94	33.
Barley	16.15	69.
Oats	36.30	91.
Corn, Grain	70.	200.

	Average	Possible
Corn Ensilage— (Tons)	12.	19.
Peas	15.33	37.
Beans	18.79	(?).
Potatoes	119.40	450.
Turnips	421.81	1000.

By "possible" is meant the actual results which have been obtained by our Experimental Farms and by many farmers. These "possibles" have been obtained under intensive cultivation methods and conditions not altogether possible on the average farm, yet they suggest the great possibilities of increased production. By greater care in the selection of seed, more thorough cultivation, fertilization, better drainage, the average could be raised by at least one-third. That in itself would add at least $150,000,000 to the annual income of Canada from the farm. It would be a great service to the Empire, and this is the year in which to do it.

Have You Attended Your District Conference?

If you have, you know that you heard once more the same old gospel of crop production. Have you talked over with your neighbour farmers the problems discussed at the Conference? If there are any questions on which you are at all doubtful write at once for information to the Canadian Department of Agriculture, Ottawa, or to your Provincial Department of Agriculture. They will be pleased to help you.

Increase Your Live Stock

Breeding stock are to-day Canada's most valuable asset. The one outstanding feature of the world's farming is that there will soon be a great shortage of meat supplies. Save your breeding stock. Plan to increase your live stock. Europe and the United States, as well as Canada, will pay higher prices for beef, mutton, and bacon in the very near future. Do not sacrifice now. Remember that live stock is the only basis for prosperous agriculture. You are farming, not speculating.

Make use of the Free Bulletins issued by the Canadian Department of Agriculture. They are mines of valuable information. The Government has nothing to sell and its reports are unbiased. There are special bulletins on wheat, oats, corn, barley, peas, beans, potatoes, turnips, onions and live stock. Send coupon below (no stamp on envelope necessary).

Canadian Department of Agriculture, Ottawa, Canada

Publications Branch, Canadian Department of Agriculture, Ottawa.

Please send bulletins on wheat, oats, corn, barley, peas, beans, potatoes, turnips, onions and live stock.

(Mark out Bulletins you do NOT want.)

Name..................................

P.O. Address ....

County .. ..Prov..................

PATRIOTISM and PRODUCTION

"Looking at the situation in even its most favorable light, there will be a demand for food that the world will find great difficulty in supplying."

HON. MARTIN BURRELL, Minister of Agriculture.

Great Britain Needs Food

VEGETABLE growers can render a real service to the Empire by increasing the production of vegetables, especially those that can readily be stored and transported. The war in Europe has devastated thousands of vegetable-producing acres and made it difficult for Britain to obtain her usual supplies. Vegetable growers are urged to select carefully the best varieties of seed and plant in properly cultivated and fertilized soil. Work hand in hand with the agricultural specialists of both the Canadian Department of Agriculture and your Provincial Department.

POTATOES
There is no farm crop the yield of which, perhaps, can be increased so much as potatoes. Potatoes have been grown in a small plot at the rate of over 700 bushels per acre at the Central Experimental Farm, Ottawa. So great is the difference in the yield of varieties that while one gave this large yield, another, under same conditions, gave but 154 bushels. It will thus be seen how important it is to plant a productive variety.

BEANS
The fact that beans have been a good price for a number of years, and also that they are of very great food value, should encourage every person who can to grow beans. Western market prices will not be influenced this year by foreign beans, and for that reason we should produce a bumper crop. The world will need them.

To the farmer's wife, the Government makes a special appeal. In many cases the vegetable garden and the poultry are largely under her direct management. Anything that she can do to increase production will be so much aid given to the Empire.

POULTRY and EGGS
Up to the commencement of the year, Great Britain imported from Belgium, France, Russia, Germany and Austria-Hungary poultry to the value of $3,000,000 per year and eggs amounting to 136,000,000 doz. Canada in 1914 imported $200,000 more poultry than she exported and imported $2,500,000 more eggs than exported. Canada needs 1,500,000 more hens, averaging 100 eggs per year, to supply the home demand before having any eggs for export. The average egg yield per hen in Canada is but 80 eggs per year, which is very low. Careful selection, feeding and housing could in a few years bring the average up to 180 eggs per hen per year. It would be a profitable thing to strive for.

LIVE STOCK
Breeding stock are today Canada's most valuable asset. The one outstanding feature of the world's farming is that there will soon be a great shortage of meat supplies. Save your breeding stock. Plan to increase your live stock. Europe and the United States, as well as Canada, will pay higher prices for beef, mutton, and bacon in the very near future. Do not sacrifice now.

Remember that live stock is the only basis for a prosperous agriculture. You are farming, not speculating

It has been said that European farmers farm better than they know; Canadian and American farmers not as well as they know. Let us this year live up to what we know. Let our contribution to the "Patriotism and Production" campaign be bumper crops.

VACANT LOTS
This call and this opportunity are not for farmers only. Residents of towns and cities can help the Empire by growing vegetables on small plots or raising chickens in their back yards. City Councils, Boards of Trade, and other organizations can help by arranging for the cultivation of vacant lots, which will relieve the unemployment situation at the same time. Those at home have a duty to perform as well as those in the firing line. From the interest manifested by the people in the "Patriotism and Production" announcements, we feel sure every one has good intentions. What we urge is that these good intentions be carried into action. Get busy. Every extra bushel you grow means that much more for export.

Canadian
Department of
Agriculture,
Ottawa, Canada

++
No Postage Required.
Publications Branch, Canadian Department of Agriculture, Ottawa.

Please send me Bulletins relating to Potatoes, Field Roots, Egg Production, Live Stock and Small Plot Culture. Mark out Bulletins you do NOT want.

Name..

P.O. Address...

County.................................Prov................... 16
++

PRODUCTION is PATRIOTISM

Back Yards and Vacant Lots

THE EMPIRE'S CALL TO FEED YOURSELVES

The farmers are responding in their thousands to the call of the Empire for greater production. They have realized that every bushel raised means a bushel more for export to Britain: that this is one way of displaying patriotism. With favorable weather, Canada's crops this year will be the greatest in her history; far greater than any of us thought possible a year ago.

Now, to round out the scheme requires equally patriotic action in the towns and cities. The people of every community, large and small, should make vacant lots and back yards productive by raising their own vegetables and garden stuff. Every pound raised, remember, is another pound furnished toward Britain's needs.

Send for the Government Bulletin

This Department will forward free a special bulletin entitled "The Vegetable Garden." The simple instructions are easy to follow and make success practically certain, even to those without experience. The best methods of cultivation for the following vegetables are fully described:— Tomatoes, Onions, Cabbage, Cauliflower, Celery, Melons, Watermelons, Cucumbers, Squash, Pumpkins, Carrots, Parsnips, Beets, Turnips, Salsify (or Oyster Plant), Radish, Peas, Beans, Corn, Egg Plant, Peppers, Spinach, Lettuce, Parsley, Sweet Herbs, Asparagus, Rhubarb.

You will enjoy amateur gardening, and profit in health and pocket as well. Children are immensely benefited, get a liberal education in the most practical manner, have outdoor amusement away from the street, become the possessors of rich red blood, strong lungs, alert minds.

Identify yourself with the national movement. Be a grower. Send for the bulletin and get your neighbors to do the same; everybody will benefit by the friendly rivalry thus started. No stamp is required on your envelope, for your coupon is truly "On His Majesty's Service."

What Local Civic Bodies Can Do

City and town councils, boards of trade, charitable bodies, women's clubs, horticultural societies, civic improvement leagues and other organizations working for the common good can accomplish a great deal locally by identifying themselves with the movement and energetically furthering it by every means at their disposal.

It will mean a thorough and permanent clean-up without cost to the community, a partial solution of the unemployed problem, and

the institution of a genuine up-lift work. Vegetables and flowers will make better citizens.

This Department has formulated a plan telling how the various civic organizations may be brought together to further this worthy aim, and giving suggestions how to launch and carry on the work to a successful issue. Write at once for the form of organization and get your community properly started in performing its share of "Greater Production."

| Canadian Department of Agriculture, Ottawa, Can. | No Postage Required. Publications Branch, Canadian Department of Agriculture, Ottawa, Canada. Please send me Bulletin entitled "The Vegetable Garden." Name...................................... Address.. Town or City.... ....Prov.........17 |

PART I
Dominion Department of Agriculture

INFORMATION SUPPLIED BY OFFICIALS OF THE VARIOUS
BRANCHES REPRESENTED

THE DOMINION EXPERIMENTAL FARMS

THE DIVISION OF HORTICULTURE

*GROWING POTATOES FOR HOME AND MARKET
BY W. T. MACOUN, DOMINION HORTICULTURIST

WHEN the farmer sows, or plants his seed his object should be to get the largest return from the soil. This can be obtained only by the use of good seed and by thorough cultivation; and there is no farm crop the yield of which can be increased so much by these methods as the potato. Potatoes have been grown in a small plot at the rate of over 700 bushels per acre at the Central Experimental Farm, Ottawa, Canada, but so great is the difference in the yield of varieties that while one gave this large yield, another, planted at the same time and in the same kind of soil, yielded only 154 bushels. It will thus be seen how important it is to plant a productive variety.

VARIETIES AND SOURCE OF SEED

A variety which is productive in one place may not be productive in another. In some places the season is too short for the later varieties, and as a result the crop is small. A variety which at one time did well in a certain locality may become

*From Agricultural War Book.

unprofitable through being diseased or becoming weak in vitality owing to unfavourable seasons. In such a case a change of seed is very desirable. As showing the advantage of a change of seed, it may be stated that new seed potatoes of eleven varieties from the Experimental Farm, Indian Head, Sask., grown at the Central Experimental Farm, Ottawa, yielded on the average at the rate of 368 bushels per acre, while seed potatoes of the same varieties which had been weakened in vitality at Ottawa by unfavourable seasons averaged only 97 bushels per acre. Other striking results could be given from seed from other provinces. Seed from the cooler and moister districts usually gives better crops the following year than seed from the warmer and drier ones. Potatoes which are immature when dug will usually give better crops the following year than potatoes which have been either prematurely ripened by hot, dry weather or even that are well ripened normally. It pays to import seed from cooler to warmer climates, as has been learned from experience. Some of the most reliable early varities are Irish Cobbler, Rochester Rose and Early Ohio, and of medium or later varieties, Carman No. 1, Gold Coin, Empire State, Green Mountain and Wee MacGregor. British varieties which have done exceptionally well in Canada are Table Talk and Davies' Warrior.

CONDITION OF SEED WHEN PLANTED

The condition the potatoes are in when the time for planting arrives is very important. If possible, potatoes should be prevented from sprouting before they are planted, unless sprouted in the light as described later on; and to prevent sprouting it is desirable to keep them in a cool cellar where the temperature does not go much above 35 degrees F. nor below 33 degrees F. The cooler potatoes are kept without freezing the better. When potatoes are kept in a warm, moist cellar, as they so often are, they sprout and the shoots take from the tubers both plant food and moisture, and as these sprouts are usually broken when handling the potatoes, the new shoots which are made when the potato starts to grow in the field have less moisture and less plant food to draw upon, and do not make as vigorous a growth as they otherwise would, and the yield is smaller. The best results will be obtained if the sets are planted immediately after cutting but if the seed is prepared several days beforehand it will pay well to coat the sets with land plaster or gypsum which will prevent evaporation. The seed potatoes should be free from disease. When potatoes are affected with the "Rhizoctonia" or "Little Potato" disease or the "Common Scab" the following treatment is recommended before the potatoes are cut or planted:—Soak the tubers for three hours in a 1 to 2000 solution of bichloride of mercury (corrosive sublimate) or in 1 pound formalin in 30 imperial gallons of water. As the former chemical is very poisonous and will corrode iron

vessels, wooden barrels or tubs should be used. Formalin is not so poisonous but should be used with care.

KINDS OF SETS TO USE

Many experiments have been tried to determine the best kinds of sets to plant, and on the average it has been found that good marketable tubers cut into pieces so as to have at least three good eyes to a piece are the best. If cut sets are found to dry up after planting, use whole potatoes for seed. It has been found to be a great advantage to "sprout" potatoes in order to have the tubers ready for use earlier than when treated in the ordinary way, and where the season is short to obtain large crops. Medium sized potatoes are selected before they have begun to sprout and placed in single layers in shallow boxes or trays, with the seed end up. The boxes are then put in a bright, airy, cool place where the temperature is low enough to prevent sprouting. After a few days the potatoes will turn green and the skin become tougher. The potatoes are now given a little more heat, but still kept in a bright place. From the seed end will now develop two or three strong sprouts, and the meaning of exposing the potatoes at first to toughen the skin is now apparent, for most of the eyes do not sprout, and practically the whole strength of the potato is concentrated in the few sprouts at the end. This is what is desired, as the fewer sprouts there are the larger proportion of marketable potatoes there will be in the crop from them. The potatoes are planted whole. If the potatoes are given plenty of light and the place where they are kept fairly cool, the sprouts will become very sturdy and strongly attached to the tuber, and will not be broken off in handling, unless very carelessly used. Tubers will develop more quickly from sprouts made slowly in a bright, cool place than from sprouts which have grown rapidly in a dark place, and, furthermore, the yields will be much heavier. Potatoes which sprout in the dark are very difficult to handle as the sprouts break off very easily. It is not absolutely necessary to place the potatoes with the seed ends up, as very satisfactory results are obtained even when potatoes are emptied indiscriminately into shallow boxes or trays and then treated as already described. The sprout should be about two inches in length at time of planting. If longer the sets are more difficult to handle.

SOIL

The most suitable soil for potatoes is a rich, deep, friable, warm sandy loam with good natural drainage, a constant though not too great a supply of moisture, and well supplied with decayed or decaying vegetable matter. They will, however, succeed well on a great variety of soils. The warmest and best drained soils that can be obtained should be chosen for the early potatoes, and the sets in this case should be planted shallow, so that they will get the advantage of the heat from the surface soil.

PREPARATION OF THE SOIL

The more thoroughly the soil is prepared the better the results will be. Loose, well pulverised soil is particularly desirable for potatoes. While heavy manuring with barnyard manure is not recommended for potatoes, the use of a moderate quantity is advised. A good way to apply this is on clover sod in autumn; the sod and manure to be turned under in the spring. If manure is used in the spring it should be well rotted and mixed with the soil, not put in the drills with the potatoes. Chemical fertilizers, if used, should be applied at the rate of 500 to 800 pounds or more per acre, in the proportion of 250 pounds of nitrate of soda, 350 pounds superphosphate, and 200 pounds sulphate of potash or muriate of potash per acre. This should be mixed with the soil in the drills.

PLANTING

As a slight frost will injure the tops, planting should be delayed to within a week of the time when the last frost is likely to occur, but in some districts potatoes may be planted later than in others. Where extra early potatoes are desired chances are taken and potatoes are planted earlier; and, should a frost threaten, the young plants, if they are above the ground, may be protected by covering them with soil. The best results have been obtained in Canada by planting the potato sets four to five inches deep for the main crop, and twelve to fourteen inches apart in rows two and one-half feet apart. As has already been stated, potatoes planted early, or if planted in soil which is too wet and cold for best results, may be planted shallower, say an inch deep, where the soil is warmer than it is further down. The sets should be covered as soon as possible after planting, so that they will not dry in the sun.

CULTIVATION

In field culture much time will be saved in hoeing later in the season if the soil is harrowed, to destroy weeds, just as the potatoes are beginning to come up, and at this time many weeds will have germinated. If the potatoes are in a garden it may be raked over for the same purpose. As a rule, the crop of potatoes will increase in proportion to the number of times the potatoes are cultivated during the growing season. There was found to be an increase of 40 bushels per acre in a crop of potatoes cultivated six times over those cultivated three times. Level cultivation will sometimes give better results than moulding or hilling up, and sometimes the results are not so good. Where the soil is stiff, or where the soil is wet, moulding, or ridging, is desirable but where the soil is loose and liable to suffer from drought in a dry time, level culture is recommended. Where the soil is both loose and moist and where the climate is moist, ridging will usually give best results. As the crop of potatoes will be much larger if the tops can be kept green until frost than if they are destroyed by insects or diseases in summer, it is important, in addition to thorough cultivation, to protect the tops from injury.

PROTECTION OF PLANTS FROM IN-
SECTS AND DISEASES

The Colorado potato beetle and the cucumber flea beetle are the commonest insects which injure the potato tops. The former can be readily killed with Paris green in the proportion of 8 ounces to 12 ounces to a forty gallon barrel of water, or with arsenate of lead in the proportion of 2 to 3 pounds to 40 gallons of water. Paris green kills quicker than arsenate of lead but the latter adheres better than Paris green, hence a mixture of both in the proportion of 8 ounces of Paris green and 1½ pounds of arsenate of lead to 40 gallons of water will kill quickly and adhere well to the foliage. These poisons will, to some extent, check the cucumber flea beetle, but in addition to them, a better preventive is a covering of Bordeaux mixture on the foliage. The Bordeaux mixture should also be used to control the early and late blights of potatoes, the latter disease causing rot. These are two of the commonest diseases. To control the early and late blight of potatoes spraying with Bordeaux mixture should be begun before the disease appears and the plants kept covered until autumn. It is safer to start spraying with Bordeaux mixture when spraying

for the potato beetles. The poison of the latter may be mixed with the Bordeaux. From three to four sprayings or more will be required, the number depending on the weather. Taking the average of three years, the increase of yield from spraying with Bordeaux mixture was at the rate of 94 bushels per acre. In some years it is much larger. The importance of keeping plants growing as late as possible is well illustrated in an experiment where the total crop of marketable potatoes per acre when dug on September 1st was 234 bushels per acre, whereas in the same field the same variety yielded 353 bushels marketable potatoes per acre when left undug until September 22nd, or in three weeks the crop had increased by 119 bushels per acre of marketable potatoes. Bordeaux mixture is made in the proportion of 6 pounds bluestone, 4 pounds lime and 40 gallons of water. Spraying mixtures should be used at the proper time and thoroughly, if good results are to be expected.

DIGGING AND STORING

Potatoes should be dug in dry weather, so that they will be dry when they are taken into the cellar. If they are diseased, the disease will not spread so rapidly among dry potatoes. If the potatoes are known to be diseased in the field, it is best to leave them in the ground as long as possible, so that diseased potatoes may more readily be seen and separated from sound ones before they are taken into the cellar. Potatoes should be stored for best results in a dry, cool, well ventilated cellar and kept at a temperature between 33 degrees F. and 35 degrees F., if possible.

Dr. F. Torrance, Veterinary Director General, announces that the Department of Agriculture is now in a position to favourably consider the issuing of permits for the importation of cattle, sheep and swine from any part of the United Kingdom.

THE DIVISION OF BOTANY

THE CONTROL OF POTATO DISEASES
'BY H. T. GÜSSOW, DOMINION BOTANIST

IT is a difficult matter to give an actual estimate of the annual losses for the Dominion due to plant diseases affecting the potato crop. Judging from the considerable number of cases, the total loss must be enormous in some years particularly.

The loss from the so-called "storage rots" amounted in some cases to 40 per cent. The yield, owing to the use of diseased seed, as far as can be judged from "misses" in the fields, has been occasionally reduced by some 30 per cent, and diseases affecting the growing plant may also cause considerable damage to the crop.

In order to prevent such loss and make the cultivation of potatoes more profitable, it is necessary to strictly follow certain lines laid down for the elimination of diseases, when it is reasonable to expect that the diseases will be eventually exterminated or reduced to a minimum. Any objections a farmer may have to carrying out the following suggestions will disappear when he finds from experience that their observance results in a greatly increased yield and higher profits to himself.

THE DISEASES OF THE SEED TUBER

1. The presence of powdery scab shall disqualify any lot of potatoes for seed purposes. Powdery scab occurs in the Maritime Provinces; no cases of this disease have been observed west of the province of Quebec. In order to prevent the dissemination of this disease, all potatoes grown in the "infested area" are being officially inspected and certified before shipment.

2. Potatoes entirely free from all diseases or blemishes are the ideal potatoes for seed purposes.

3. When selecting potatoes for planting, all bruised, decayed, externally diseased or unsound tubers should be removed.

4. Tubers showing common scab should, preferably, be all removed. The chances are that scabby seed will produce a scabby crop.

5. After having removed all externally diseased and otherwise injured tubers, the seed should be soaked in bags or bulk for three hours in a solution of bichloride of mercury, 1 part in 2,000 parts of water. After treatment, spread out and dry.

6. When dry, cutting the potatoes for "sets" will commence. Provide each person engaged with a potato knife, and keep a number of knives in a wooden pail containing a solution of 1: 1,000 bichloride of mercury.

7. The stem end of the tuber is the seat of several internal diseases. Cut a thin slice off the stem end of each potato; if perfectly sound and free from brown streaks, rings or spots, continue cutting it up to required size.

8. Discard at once all tubers showing discolouration, when cut as above, at the stem end, and throw out those showing any kind of spotting inside, though the stem end itself may have shown no disease.

9. Having used the knife on a tuber showing any kind of discolouration inside, throw it at once into the disinfecting solution, and take out another knife before cutting up a new tuber. A knife that has cut through a diseased tuber conveys certain diseases to the new tuber, hence it is very important to change the knife after having thrown out a diseased tuber. It is waste of time to cut out brown spots and use the rest of the tuber.

After following these precautions, everything has been done to eliminate diseases conveyed by unsound seed potatoes. The sets are now ready for planting.

DISEASE-INFECTED LAND

In the case of powdery scab and a number of other potato diseases, the causal organism persists in the soil for a number of years; it is, therefore, necessary to avoid too frequent succession of potato crops. Ordinarily, potatoes should not be grown oftener on the same land than every fourth year. Where powdery scab has existed, it is advisable to change to land that has not previously produced a diseased crop of potatoes. The infected land may be used for any other crop with the exception of potatoes.

THE DISEASES OF THE GROWING PLANT

The recognition of diseases noticeable only in the growing plant will invariably be most difficult. Where doubt exists, a specimen showing the suspected trouble should be mailed to the Dominion Botanist for his advice, but, generally speaking, careful attention to the elimination of disease in the seed tubers will have largely reduced the disease affecting the growing plant. Farmers should make it a rule to immediately remove any individual hill that may show signs of yellowing, curling-up of leaves or otherwise feeble growth, as well as any individual plant with flowers of a different colour from the rest, in order to keep varieties pure.

SPRAYING

1. Spraying is practised for two main reasons: First, to control the Colorado beetle; and, second, to control Late Blight. There are other minor reasons.

2. Experiments have shown that several solutions will destroy the Colorado beetle, but the solution acting most rapidly is the one to use.

3. Spraying must be done thoroughly. All plants, and all parts thereof, must be well covered. A plant with one half sprayed and the other half missed will have the unsprayed part eaten off by the beetles very quickly. This will leave enough beetles to continue the pest. One spray thoroughly applied is better than several carelessly applied.

4. We recommend two special applications for beetles; one when the plants are from four to six inches high, to be followed by another from one to two weeks later. The interval between the sprays will naturally vary according to the severity of attack. The solution we use and recommend is made up as follows :—

Eight to 10 ounces of Paris green, 1½ to 2 pounds arsenate of lead to 40 imperial gallons of water.

This solution adheres satisfactorily to the foliage and controls the ravages of the beetle. Spraying will generally commence towards the 1st of July.

5. After the first two applications have been made, we continue spraying regularly once every two weeks right up to harvest time, using "poisonous" Bordeaux mixture of the following composition:—

Four pounds of lime or more, if necessary; 6 pounds sulphate of copper, 12 ounces Paris green, 40 imperial gallons of water.

6. Do not spray on very windy days. Spray early in the morning, or commence two hours before sunset. Postpone spraying in unsettled weather, but spray thoroughly, particularly after a period of rain.

EDUCATION AS AN AID IN THE CONTROL OF PLANT DISEASES

BY W. A. McCUBBIN, FIELD LABORATORY OF PLANT PATHOLOGY, ST. CATHERINES, ONT

IN the course of two years' association with the work of plant diseases in the Niagara peninsula, and southern Ontario, it has become increasingly apparent that, aside from the small percentage of farmers who have attended agricultural colleges, there are comparatively few who have an adequate knowledge of the nature of the diseases which affect their crops. Even where control measures are practised, there is often haziness and misconception as to the cause of the trouble; whereas with a more definite knowledge of the principles of disease, such measures could be carried out in a more intelligent and satisfactory manner. With a view to supplying this lack, and to give an accurate if limited knowledge of the fundamental features concerned in diseases, a series of addresses was arranged to be given during the winter. Each lecture was well illustrated with lantern slides, some sixty of which had been prepared for the purpose in the field laboratory at St. Catharines.

In these addresses a distinction was drawn between the diseases caused by parasites and those injuries arising from the action of physical, chemical, or climatic agencies. Attention was also directed to the obscure and little known troubles usually classed as physiological diseases. In regard to parasitic diseases, use was made of numerous illustrations to present a clear picture of the important phases in the life history of a fungus. The minute size and vast number of the spores of fungi were estimated by simple calculations, and the means by which these spores are disseminated were pointed out. Then the problem of infection was dealt with, especially in reference to those factors which favour or limit infection. In order to present a general view of diseases, a series of slides of various types of parasitic diseases were shown, as well as a number illustrative of physiological diseases and injuries due to external causes. When time permitted, the methods employed in controlling diseases were discussed and questions answered concerning these.

During the winter such addresses were given to twelve agricultural classes in various counties; to three meetings of farmers' institutes; to a special audience of fruit growers and farmers in St. Catharines; to the Lincoln county teachers' convention; to the science students of the St. Catharines collegiate; to the scholars and ratepayers of three schools in Lincoln county, and to a men's club of St. Catharines.

The attention and interest shown in these addresses have been a great encouragement in this work, and it is hoped to have them continued and extended during the coming winter.

THE DIVISION OF APICULTURE

THE BEE KEEPING SITUATION IN CANADA

BY F. W. L. SLADEN, APIARIST, EXPERIMENTAL FARMS SYSTEM

THE present deplorable war has had the effect of increasing the value of certain staple articles of food and reducing the value of certain luxuries. Honey being something between a necessity and a luxury has not been much affected in price by war conditions, though it has been affected by the price of other things and the usual fluctuating market. At the present time, owing to the poor honey crop in Ontario in 1914 and the abnormally high price of sugar, the price of honey is good and it behooves every bee-keeper to do his utmost to produce a large crop of honey in 1915. With proper distribution the demand for extracted honey in Canada is excellent, but the demand for comb honey, which is more of a luxury, is limited. With a given number of bees about double as much extracted

the honey can be kept good in such a package for any reasonable length of time if stored in a dry place.

It is, in a sense, regrettable that in the temperate region of North America, owing partly to the superior quality of the honey produced and the high cost of living, the cost of honey is higher than elsewhere, because this, with the duty on honey entering Canada (3 cents per lb., and 7½ per cent ad valorem from the United States, etc., and 2 cents per lb. with 5 per cent ad valorem from countries enjoying the British

WINTERING BEES OUT-OF-DOORS AT THE CENTRAL EXPERIMENTAL FARM, OTTAWA, IN CASES HOLDING FOUR HIVES EACH AND PACKED WITH PLANER SHAVINGS.

honey as comb honey can be produced, and the production of extracted honey is easier because swarming can be more readily controlled. It will, therefore, be seen that it generally pays better to produce extracted honey than comb honey, and the present conditions somewhat accentuate this dictum. The best package for extracted honey in commercial quantities is the 5 lb. and 10 lb. tin honey "pail." The cost of this package is much less than that of glass jars in comparison with the value of the honey content, and

preferential tariff) makes the price of honey in Canada so high that it practically prohibits the exportation of Canadian honey. Nevertheless these conditions make intelligent beekeeping very profitable in good regions and seasons.

Among the great variety of grades of honey produced in Canada two may be singled out : (1) clover honey produced from white Dutch clover (*Trifolium repens*) and alsike clover (*T. hybridum*), plants which grow abundantly, wild and cultivated, in all the farming regions of

Canada excepting the drier portions of the prairies, and (2) fire-weed (*Epilobium angustifolium*) honey gathered from the great willow herb or fireweed, a common weed in forest clearings, especially after devastation by fire, and often abundant in certain places in the north. Up to the present time clover honey has been by far the most important commercial product and its quality in the opinion of most consumers is unexcelled, but its production is rendered uncertain from year to year by drought and other causes. On the make beekeeping in Canada a very profitable industry and it might be engaged in very much more than it is at present. The outcry about a slight fall in price by some of the extensive beekeepers in Ontario when a large crop of clover honey is harvested is hardly well founded, for the markets in the Prairie Provinces are large and growing, and honey has a ready sale in all villages everywhere if put up cleanly in neat packages. Besides, extracted honey will keep properly stored, from year to year, without deterioration. It is only by

APIARY AT THE DOMINION EXPERIMENTAL STATION, STE. ANNE DE LA POCATIÈRE.

other hand, fireweed honey, though somewhat insipid in flavour, is little affected by weather conditions and enormous crops of it have been harvested in apiaries situated where much fireweed grows. A maximum of 500 lb. of honey, mainly from this source, was taken from one hive in the bush twenty miles north of Maniwaki, P.Q., in 1914.

In general it may be said that the abundance of nectar producing flowers, the long summer season, the usually sufficient rainfall and the comparatively high price of honey an abundant display of honey in our stores that the present demand for it will continue and increase.

The three principal problems in beekeeping:—swarming, disease and wintering, are all capable of successful solution with care, and what is most needed at present is intelligent and careful methods of beekeeping. Our public schools are turning out men and women that will read our publications and make use of the information contained therein, decimation by disease is, in some districts, eliminating the neglectful keeper of bees in old-fashioned box-hives, and the Provincial Governments, have and are doing good educational work through their bee-diseases inspectors, appointed through the bee disease laws that have been passed in most of the provinces. Mention should also be made of the beekeepers' associations, some of which are showing much activity and usefulness.

THE FRUIT BRANCH

MARKETING THE PEACH CROP

BY C. W. BAXTER, CHIEF FRUIT INSPECTOR FOR EASTERN ONTARIO AND QUEBEC

OWING to the increased planting of peach trees in Ontario during the past few years, many of which will come into bearing this season, and owing to the anticipated large- yield from the older trees, it is expected that the 1915 peach crop will be large.

The killing of the peach buds during the winter of 1913-14 was followed by an excellent growing season. The result was that the trees went into last winter under ideal conditions and with a large increase in the number of fruit spurs. Reports received up to date show that the trees have wintered well. There has been no killing of the buds by frost and should nothing of a serious nature occur it is reasonable to predict a crop which will be the largest in the history of Canada.

The peach growers of Ontario experienced difficulties in marketing the large crop of 1913 and many marketed their fruit at a loss. It is necessary, on account of the very perishable nature of peaches, that the crop be moved quickly and it is obvious that some provision be made to obtain a wider and more systematic distribution if the difficulties experienced in 1913 are to be avoided in 1915.

With this object in view, the writer was instructed by Mr. D. Johnson, Dominion Fruit Commissioner, to visit the peach growing sections in the state of Georgia, to enquire into the methods employed in marketing Georgia peaches and to secure any other information which might be applicable and of value to fruit growers in Canada.

Although much has been accomplished by co-operative associations, and although some individual efforts have proved successful, yet there is not to-day in eastern Canada a central organization specially engaged in marketing tender fruits. When the peach crop is heavy, the large consuming centres are usually flooded with fruit, which means ruinous prices to the grower. At the same time many of the smaller towns and villages are paying such high prices that the consumption is materially lessened.

To successfully market a large crop of peaches it is necessary to make an early estimate of the total crop, to employ methods which will increase consumption and to take the necessary steps to secure a wide and even distribution. The Georgia Fruit Exchange has accomplished these and other things for the peach growers of that state. This organization is an incorporated body organized primarily for the purpose of selling and marketing fruit and vegetables, but, owing to the great increase in the production of peaches during the past few years, efforts are now practically confined to the marketing of that fruit.

In 1910 the Georgia Fruit Exchange marketed in only 80 cities. In 1914 this number was increased to 197. Previous to this extension of markets over 80 per cent of the total crop was shipped to three centres, which were overstocked, little or no profit was returned to the producers.

In 1914 the same organization handled 68 per cent of the total crop. The fact that 197 cities and towns were supplied, enabled individual shippers to obtain much better prices at the same three centres mentioned above. For example, 29 per cent of the total crop was shipped to New York City. Of these shipments only 18 per cent were made by the Exchange and 52 per cent by individual shippers. Forty-three per cent of the total crop was shipped to three other cities, and of this fruit 28 per cent was shipped by the Exchange and 76 per cent by private individuals.

Wider distribution is essential in the marketing of the Canadian peach crop. It will result in better prices for the producer and will be a guarantee of lower prices to the consumers, as a whole.

A pamphlet dealing with the marketing of peaches in Georgia will shortly be issued by the Fruit Commissioner's Branch, and will be mailed free to any grower requesting same.

NOTES

While in eastern Canada during the early part of the year, Mr. A. H. Flack, Chief Fruit Inspector for the Prairie Provinces, gave demonstrations in the box-packing of apples at Truro, Berwick, Port Williams, Middleton and Kentville in Nova Scotia, Woodstock in New Brunswick and La Trappe in Quebec.

Following this series of meetings Mr. Flack went to Ontario where he assisted Mr. P. J. Carey, Dominion apple packing expert, at similar demonstrations in box and barrel packing at the following points:— Forest (February 9-13), Trenton (February 15), Wellington (February 16), Bowmanville (February 17), and Goderich (February 18 and 19).

All the meetings were well attended and much interest was shown by those present.

Mr. P. J. Carey has also given demonstrations in orchard management, box and barrel packing, at the following places in Ontario:—Simcoe (February 22 and 23), Ancaster (February 24), Waterdown (February 25), and Strathroy (February 26).

A better method in seed selection would mean millions of dollars in the increase of production.—*Prof. C. A. Zavitz.*

THE ENTOMOLOGICAL BRANCH

THE CONTROL OF CUTWORMS

BY ARTHUR GIBSON, CHIEF ASSISTANT ENTOMOLOGIST, IN CHARGE OF VEGETABLE, STORED PRODUCTS AND GREENHOUSE INSECT INVESTIGATIONS

DURING the months of May and June remedies for the various destructive species of cutworms are urgently requested by farmers, market gardeners, fruit growers, etc. Many of our common cutworms pass the winter in a partially grown condition and in spring as soon as young seedling plants appear above ground or when such

THE RED-BACKED CUTWORM, *EUXOA OCHROGASTER*—ENLARGED ONE-QUARTER. (Original).

plants as cabbages and cauliflowers are transplanted in the field, many are cut or eaten off near the surface of the ground, or a little below it. In many instances the young plant will be found to have been drawn partly into the ground. Not all cutworms, however, feed in this manner; some climb up fruit trees or such plants as currants, gooseberries, tomatoes, etc., and feed upon the foliage or the fruit. In fact, when they are excessively abundant they will attack anything green and juicy. In years of abundance some kinds, such as the Variegated cutworm, the Spotted cutworm, and the Black Army cutworm, assume the marching habit, so characteristic of the true Army-worm.

The poisoned bran remedy is the one which is now used most extensively for the destruction of cutworms generally. This is made by moistening the bran with sweetened water and then dusting in Paris green in the proportion of half a pound of Paris green to fifty pounds of bran. It is important that the bran be noticeably moistened (but not made into a mash or moistened too much to prevent its being crumbled through the fingers) so that when the poison is added, it will adhere to practically every particle. Two gallons of water, in which half a pound of sugar has been dissolved, is sufficient to moisten fifty pounds of bran. If more convenient, the same quantity of salt may be used instead of sugar, or even molasses may be employed. The mixture should be applied thinly as soon as cutworm injury is noticed. It is important, too, that the mixture be scattered after sundown, so that it will be in the very best condition when the cutworms come out to feed at night. This material is very attractive to them and when they crawl about in search of food they will actually eat it in preference to

YOUNG TOMATOES DESTROYED BY THE VARIEGATED CUTWORM, *PERIDROMA SAUCIA*. (Original).

the growing vegetation. If the mixture is put out during a warm day, it soon becomes dry and is not, of course, as attractive to the cutworms. In treating fields of hoed crops, such as beets, turnips, etc., a simple method is to have a sack filled with the bran, hung about the neck and by walking between two rows, and using both hands, the mixture may be scattered along the row on either side. When cutworms are so numerous as to assume the walking habit, the poisoned bran may be spread just ahead of their line of march. In gardens, where vegetables or

TOPS OF GLADIOLI SHOWING HABIT OF CUT-WORMS IN CUTTING OFF YOUNG PLANTS, AND ALSO INJURY TO TENDER LEAVES ABOVE GROUND. MANY FLOWERING PLANTS WERE DESTROYED IN THIS MAN-NER IN 1914. (Original).

flowering plants are to be protected, a small quantity of the material may be put around, but not touching each plant. Fruit trees may be protected from climbing cutworms in the same way, but the mixture should, of course, not be thrown in quantity against the base of the tree, otherwise injury may result from the possible

burning effect of the Paris green. As an instance of the remarkable effectiveness of the poisoned bran, I would mention that on one occasion when we used it to protect young tobacco plants on the Central Experimental Farm, we soon afterwards made careful counts of the dead cutworms near a number of the plants. Around one plant we found 17 dead cutworms, around another 8, around still another 9, and so on. Only one half of the tobacco plantation was treated. In the other half where no poisoned bran had been distributed, the cutworms were extremely destructive, very many plants being destroyed.

During 1914, the Kansas grasshopper formula was found of equal value in the destruction of the Variegated cutworm and it will undoubtedly prove a most useful remedy for other cutworms, particularly the surface-feeding kinds. This formula is as follows:

Bran.....................	20 pounds.
Paris green	1 pound.
Molasses...............	2 quarts.
Oranges or lemons.........	3
Water...................	3½ gallons.

In preparing the bran mash mix the bran and Paris green thoroughly in a wash tub while dry. Squeeze the juice of the oranges or lemons into the water and chop the remaining pulp and the peel into fine bits and add them to the water. Dissolve the molasses in the water and wet the bran and poison with the mixture, stirring at the same time so as to dampen the mash thoroughly. In our experiments near Ottawa on the control of locusts the farmers prepared the mixture on the cement floor of a stable or other outhouse, stirring it thoroughly by means of an ordinary field hoe. The mixture should be broadcasted early in the evening. In the control of the Variegated cutworm in alfalfa fields in Kansas, the above quantity of bran was spread in such a manner as to treat about three acres. Scatter the mixture thinly in places where it will reach the greatest number of cutworms, and when thus spread there is no danger of birds, poultry or live stock being poisoned.

Fresh bundles of any succulent weed, grass, clover, or other tender vegetation, which have been dipped into a strong solution of Paris green (one ounce of Paris green to a pail of water), may be placed at short distances apart in an infested field, or between rows of vegetables, or roots, and will attract many cutworms and protect the crops from further injury. These bundles, also, should be put out after sundown, so that the plants will not be too withered before the cutworms find them. As in the case of the poisoned bran, they should be applied just as soon as the presence of cutworms is detected.

THE HEALTH OF ANIMALS BRANCH

TUBERCULOSIS IN SWINE

BY F. TORRANCE, B.A., D.V.SC., VETERINARY DIRECTOR GENERAL

THE loss from tuberculosis in swine is a serious one, involving not only a lessening in our food supply, but also a direct loss of money to almost everyone engaged in the hog industry. In the abattoirs under the inspection of the Health of Animals Branch of the Department of Agriculture, a careful record of all cases of tuberculosis in swine is kept. These records show that the disease is increasing in Canada, as the following figures indicate:—

PERCENTAGE OF SWINE AFFECTED WITH TUBERCULOSIS.

Year.	1910	1911	1912	1913	1914
Percent	8.90	11.60	12.69	13.41	13.72

In some parts of Canada the percentage is higher than in others, as for instance,—

	Per cent 1910	Per cent 1911	Per cent 1912	Per cent 1913	Per cent 1914
Essex Co.	16.28	21.41	21.49	26.72	28.00
Kent Co.	24.57	26.31	25.45	30.27	32.00
Ont Prov.	10.46	13.86	14.84	16.05	19.15

Every fourth or fifth hog affected with tuberculosis! Surely a state of affairs calling urgently for some attention. Fortunately for our food supply, the term "affected with tuberculosis" does not mean in every case that the hog is unfit for food.

Generally we find the disease in its early stages, and confined to one or two glands, and it is only necessary to condemn a portion of the carcass. For instance, the glands at the root of the tongue may be tuberculous, or the glands in the throat, and the rest of the carcass show no sign of disease ; the head and tongue are condemned and the rest of the carcass is passed for food. But in spite of the fact that it is the exception to condemn the whole carcass, the number of portions condemned is so large, that the aggregate of the losses amounts to a large sum, estimated for the past year at $173,671.88.

The packers have for some time been distributing this loss among the farmers by deducting one-half of one per cent from the purchase money of every lot of hogs they buy. This is justified on the ground that it is impossible to protect themselves against buying diseased hogs, as these can only be detected after slaughter, and as innocent purchasers, the packers should not have to stand the loss.

The farmer who has only healthy stock naturally objects to paying part of the loss on a neighbour's diseased pigs, and this arrangement has caused some dissatisfaction. Much of this loss and annoyance could be avoided. Hogs can be protected from tuberculosis by simple measures that any farmer can adopt, and it is probably through not *knowing how*, that the spread of the disease has not been prevented.

If the way in which swine acquire the disease is known, and this source of infection is removed, the swine will remain healthy. How then do hogs become tuberculous?

Hogs acquire tuberculosis from cattle, especially from dairy cows. Tuberculosis is a common disease of cattle. Cows affected with it often give off the germs of the disease in the manure, and sometimes in the milk. Hogs feeding in yards or pastures with cattle have the opportunity of picking out grains of corn, etc., in the manure, and thus taking the germs of tuberculosis into the system. Skim milk and whey can easily convey the germs of the disease to hogs fed partly or wholly on dairy by-products.

These two facts account for practically all the tuberculosis of hogs. It is unlikely that it spreads to any extent from hog to hog. The majority of the cases found on post-mortem examination at the abattoirs are in the early stage, showing that inspection has not reached the stage when the victim is dangerous to other hogs, or in fact capable of passing on the infection.

The practical application of this knowledge should result in keeping swine away from yards and pastures occupied by cattle, and in sterilizing all dairy by-products before feeding them to hogs. No scientific pasteurizing apparatus is required for this. Let the by-products be well boiled for a few minutes and all the protection needed is given. The trouble and expense of boiling skim milk for pigs would be repaid by the protection of their health, and as for allowing pigs to gather part of their food from the droppings of cattle, who would care to defend it?

In conclusion, I strongly advise farmers and hog raisers to keep their swine apart from cattle, and if skim milk or whey is used for feed, to have it well boiled. Tuberculosis of swine, if this advice were largely followed, would soon become much less frequent and losses would be prevented.

President W. J. Black of the Manitoba Agricultural College reports that over one hundred reeves and other municipal officers attended the lectures at the short course and convention on highway construction held in the auditorium of the College from March 3rd to 15th. Addresses were delivered by professors of the College, by the Provincial Highway Commissioner and the Minister of Public Works, by civic officials, by the president of the Manitoba Good Roads Association, by the State Engineer of Minnesota and by the Professor of Highway Engineering of Iowa State College. Those who attended were so well pleased with their experience that they passed a unanimous resolution requesting that a similar course and lectures be given next year.

Mr. W. E. Scott, Deputy Minister of Agriculture for British Columbia has issued a circular announcing that it has been decided to pay a bonus of five dollars to winners in the field crop competitions who submit a satisfactory statement of the cost of producing the crop entered for competition. This is in furtherance of the scheme to make a study of the sections of the province best adapted to certain crops.

PART II

Provincial Departments of Agriculture

INFORMATION SUPPLIED BY OR THROUGH OFFICIALS OF PROVINCIAL
DEPARTMENTS OF AGRICULTURE, INCLUDING
AGRICULTURAL COLLEGES

POTATO GROWING

PRINCE EDWARD ISLAND

BY THEODORE ROSS, SECRETARY FOR AGRICULTURE

THE potato crop of Prince Edward Island stands third in importance of field crops. Its average annual value for the last four years has been about $1,800,000, the acreage about 32,000, the yield per acre a little over 200 bushels, and the price from 20 to 30 cents per bushel. The chief varieties grown for early market are Early Rose; Early Harvest; and Beauty of Hebron, and for general crop, McIntyre; Dakota Red, and Green Mountain.

The Island is particularly adapted to potato growing as the soil is nearly all a loam or sandy loam. The general practice is to grow potatoes in a six or seven years' rotation. The pasture land is broken early in the autumn, generally the last of August or the first of September. It is rolled and harrowed at once to hasten decomposition and to germinate the weed seeds thoroughly. It is then harrowed every two or three weeks till the end of November, after which it is cross-ploughed or ribbed up. In the spring it is again harrowed, and the sets for early potatoes planted as soon as the land is fit, varying according to locality and season from the first to the second of May. The land is prepared for the general crop by further harrowing to preserve the moisture, and to destroy any remaining weeds. The planting is done from the 15th of May to the middle of June. The bulk of the crop in an average season is, however, planted by the first of June.

A large number of farmers grow a crop of oats after the pasture before the potatoes. By doing this they hope to economize labour in the preparation of the soil, and to have a better opportunity of destroying weeds.

FERTILIZATION

Barnyard manure is the principal fertilizer used. Probably artificial fertilizers are used in the growing of 25 per cent of the potatoes, but only with barnyard manure, which is very frequently made up of seaweed and kelp, swamp muck and stable manure. Where the former is very abundant, potatoes are frequently grown on it and an artificial fertilizer. It seems to improve the quality, producing a white, clean-skinned, dry potato. Pure chemicals are the only artificial fertilizers used in this province, and, as has already been

334

said, are used with farmyard manure, at the rate of about 100 lb. of nitrate, of soda, 300 lb. of superphosphate, and 150 lb. of muriate of potash per acre. Where stable manure only is used it is generally spread on the pasture field during the previous autumn and in the spring; where it is mixed with seaweed and kelp and swamp muck it is generally applied in the autumn; if the land has been in oats, before the ploughing has been done, if in sod, after, or in the spring just when the planting is being done.

The seed is generally cut a few days before planting and sprinkled with lime, and sometimes treated with corrosive sublimate.

Considerable care is taken in the selection of the tubers that are to be used for seed. The sets are cut as large as possible with either one or two eyes. The planting is generally done with the plough, the sets being dropped, every third round, from 12 to 18 inches apart in the row. There are a few potato planters in the province, but probably not more than a dozen.

The harrow is used at frequent intervals till the potatoes are about four inches high, to destroy weeds and to conserve the moisture. The scuffler is run through them, generally three times before they blossom, after which they are hilled.

The potato bug (Colorado beetle) and the blight are the chief troubles of the potato grower, for the former Paris green is applied three times during the growing season, and about half the farmers make the last two applications in conjunction with the Bordeaux mixture for the prevention of blight.

The harvesting of the early crop begins about the middle of September, and of the main crop about October 10th. The picking is generally done by a gang of from four to eight, who go from farm to farm during the digging season. The potatoes are dumped into a two-wheeled cart, and hauled direct to market or to the place of storage, which is almost always the cellar of the farm house. They are tipped into it through a hatchway and shovelled back into large bins, where they remain till they are used by the farmer himself or hauled away to market. Large quantities of them are used by the farmer for the feeding of pigs, sheep, and, if the price is low, to cattle. No steps have yet been taken by the Department of Agriculture of the Island to facilitate the marketing of potatoes.

NOVA SCOTIA
BY F. L. FULLER, SUPT. OF AGRICULTURAL SOCIETIES

A great variety of soils, widely separated markets, calling for an entirely different type of tuber, have made potato growing in the province of Nova Scotia a somewhat local matter, so that one cannot make statements in regard to varieties, etc., equally applicable to the whole province.

Following the American Civil War, when potatoes were in great demand in the United States and admitted "duty free," the farmers of the Annapolis Valley (where soil conditions were particularly favourable, and where, on account of the nearness of Boston, a great American potato buying port, and the abundance of home-built wooden vessels affording easy and cheap transportation), made a specialty of potato culture. This was prior to the appearance of the Colorado potato beetle; rot and blight were scarcely known; prices remained uniformly high for a number of years, and as a result, this portion of the province reaped a great harvest. Fortunes were accumulated, magnificent homes were built, and a habit of extravagant living was formed, which proved a decided handicap in later years. It was during this period that a variety of potatoes called "Prince Alberts" became very popular. This was a strong growing, rough, skinned, dark blue variety, and became known in Boston as Nova Scotia "Blues," "Shenangoes," and finally as "Blue Noses," a name

followed by an increase in duty to 25 cents per bushel. About this time (or to be exact, in 1877), the Colorado beetle made its appearance, and later blight and rot frequently destroyed the entire crop. Thus for a time a famous potato-growing section almost entirely dropped out of the business, developing the apple business instead. As the price of potatoes went up in the United States, the Government found it in their own interests to reduce the duty. Consequent to this change,

PRIZE-WINNING POTATO FIELD ON FARM OF ALBERT C. VERNOTTE AND SON, WEST NORTHFIELD, LUNENBURG COUNTY, NOVA SCOTIA.

which was later applied to all Nova Scotians, not merely as a nickname, but rather as a mark of quality of both the man and his products. The name with its aristocratic suggestion is still in use, and we are inclined to be proud of it, although many are unaware of its really plebeian origin.

Some years later the American government, by imposing a duty of 15 cents per bushel on potatoes, gave the industry a set-back. This was

and at the same time, the development of the West Indies' market, together with a knowledge of the means of combatting pests, the industry has again grown to quite formidable dimensions, taking second place only, and fitting in nicely with fruit growing. During the last few years the United Fruit Company, which is a very strong organization in the Annapolis Valley, have found a very remunerative market in Cuba and elsewhere for large quantities of potatoes. Meanwhile, other portions of the province, particularly Colchester, Hants and Kings counties, have had a very good, if somewhat limited, market in Bermuda. The demand here was for seed potatoes of the red-skinned varieties, and was confined almost entirely to the "Garnet Chili" variety.

Two years ago powdery scab was reported in Canada, and, as a result, an embargo was placed on our potatoes going to United States and Bermuda. The federal and provincial Departments of Agriculture took this matter up and by means of a careful inspection ascertained that powdery scab is largely confined to counties which do a coastal trade, the disease having been distributed by potatoes brought in in this manner being used for seed. Fortunately the four largest exporting counties, Colchester, Hants, Kings and Annapolis, were found to be practically free from the disease. As a result, Bermuda, which Island had declared an embargo on all Canadian potatoes, admitted potatoes from these counties, provided a certificate of inspection, certifying freedom from the disease, was attached by the plant pathologist of the provincial Department of Agriculture.

While few sections of the province grow largely for export, most counties more than supply the local demand, and many of them, by adopting improved methods, have brought the cultivation of this crop to a high state of perfection.

The Department of Agriculture, to encourage better methods, has for some years given prizes for the best acre of potatoes. For this purpose the province is divided into four districts, Annapolis, Kings, Hants and Lunenburg counties comprising one of these districts. Lunenburg county growers won the first four prizes in this competition. The first prize field, containing exactly two acres, yielded 970 bushels of market-

able potatoes, and 30 bushels of refuse, or small potatoes. Almost as high yields were recorded in the competition held in the eastern counties of the mainland.

The quality of Nova Scotia potatoes is first-class. Some years ago the Ontario Agricultural College made a cooking and starch content test of potatoes gathered from all parts of Canada, and a sample sent by the Nova Scotia Provincial Farm made the highest test, while Nova Scotia potatoes, as a whole, stood higher than those from any other province.

Regarding varieties, while there are many named varieties, they do not represent many different characteristics. During recent years the demand has been strongly for a smooth, medium sized, white potato, and in both the early and the general crop the "Carman" type largely predominates.

The place in the rotation, the preparation of the soil and the method of cultivation, differ in different localities. In sections where they are grown in large quantities the work is done entirely by machinery. In such instances, a stubble field is usually chosen. The crop is planted with a planter, cultivation done almost entirely with different styles of cultivators, and harvested with potato "diggers." In smaller fields, where hand cultivation is practised, a sod field is usually chosen. Where hand cultivation is practised, there is usually more care in the selection of seed, more fertilizer used, and much larger yields secured.

Commercial fertilizer is largely used for the growth of this crop. Where sod fields are used, it is sometimes customary to spread a dressing of stable manure on the sod and plough it under, and commercial fertilizer worked in with the harrow.

Seed is usually treated with formalin. Scarcely any of the larger growers attempt to grow this crop now without spraying. Bordeaux mixture is the most common spray in use. Where there are Potato Beetles, paris green is added to the mixture. The amount of spraying varies; all fields in the provincial competitions were sprayed from two to four times during the growing season.

Where possible, the crop is largely marketed from the field. Fruit warehouses and root cellars are used when necessary to store the crop.

NEW BRUNSWICK

BY J. B. DAGGETT, SECRETARY FOR AGRICULTURE

THE potato industry in New Brunswick has assumed large proportions in the last ten years, until the crop in 1914 amounted to approximately ten millions of bushels. Very much has been learned during these years as to the place in the rotation, preparation and cultivation of the soil, fertilizers and potato diseases.

Previous to ten years ago, commercial fertilizers were practically unknown in the province, but in recent years they have come into very general use, until at present seventy-five per cent of the potatoes raised are grown with commercial fertilizers with an increase in the crop of twenty-five to thirty-five per cent reported. The potatoes so raised are not so susceptible to scab as when raised upon ordinary barnyard manures or fish manures, such as are used in some sections of the province. It has been found that commercial fertilizers cannot be continuously used successfully without a proper rotation and by some means adding vegetable matter to the soil. Farmers who have attempted this have found that their land would soon require two thousand pounds instead of fifteen hundred pounds to the acre.

The following rotation is being adopted throughout the province: First year, potatoes with commercial fertilizer; second year, seed down with a grain crop, with a much larger proportion of clover than was formerly used; third year, hay; very many are now taking off but one crop of hay and then breaking up and ploughing under the second growth of clover; the next year a crop of corn or turnips is raised, the field having been well fertilized with barn-yard manures. This we consider a very satisfactory rotation. The same system is followed by all our farmers, except that some take off two or even three crops of hay before breaking up. From three to five years, however, is the average length of rotation among our best farmers.

While there are a number of varieties of potatoes being raised in New Brunswick, the two favourites are Irish Cobbler for the early crop and Green Mountain for the general crop.

We have the usual potato diseases common to all countries, but we are learning that the vast majority of these may be successfully combatted by the proper treatment of seed, by careful selection of all seed stock and the faithful use of the Bordeaux mixture. I would like to emphasize the word "faithful" as, in my observations, very many of our farmers are not faithful in the use of this excellent article. When the farmer persistently uses this mixture from the time the plant is a few inches above the ground until well toward the harvest, our experience has been that we have very little blight and the tubers are invariably much better keepers in storage.

The New Brunswick product is in very much better condition than it was several years ago. There is a general agreement that there has been a steady improvement and that we are turning out a very much better quality of potatoes than in the past. From a recent visit to the potato growing areas, I am satisfied that the majority of our farmers are giving close attention to the things that are necessary for the production of the very best crop. Large quantities are shipped to the market directly from the field at the time of harvesting, probably twenty-five per cent, the balance being stored either in cellars or in specially built frost-proof potato houses, used exclusively for the storing of potatoes. These buildings are light and well ventilated and are so arranged that teams can drive into them and the potatoes can be sorted and loaded in the building. They are fitted with heating apparatus that will heat the building during excessive cold. These buildings are giving splendid satisfaction.

QUEBEC

BY REV. H. BOIS, PROFESSOR OF AGRONOMY AT THE SCHOOL OF AGRICULTURE, STE. ANNE DE LA POCATIÈRE

THE area annually planted in potatoes in the province of Quebec is about 125,000 acres, yielding twenty million bushels valued at $9,500,000.

The following varieties are particularly recommended:—

Early: — Rochester-Rose, Rose-Blanche, Rose-hâtive.

Standard varieties for general use:— Carman No. 1, Late Puritan, Money Maker, Snowflake, Green Mountain, Jerusalem.

On sandy soils and loams, it is recommended to plant potatoes after a pasture. On clay lands, which are difficult to work, the pasture should be followed by a cereal, then by potatoes.

In the first case the pasture is ploughed in August, the land is harrowed then rolled; in the spring, at the end of April, the manure is ploughed under or harrowed in. In the second case, ten pounds of red clover seed are sown with the cereal; if manure is available in the fall it is spread on the top of the land; otherwise the land is manured in the spring. At the beginning of June the land is ploughed six inches deep and worked as thoroughly as possible with a disc harrow. Some growers find it preferable to plant at two different dates in order to lessen the chances of failure; a part of the potatoes is planted in May, the other part about the 15th of June. The tubers are planted with the planting machine or the plough; the rows are from 25 to 30 inches apart, according to the variety, and the sets are planted from three to four inches deep.

A few days after the potatoes are planted, the harrow is run lengthwise and crosswise to loosen the land and destroy weeds which may have come up. As soon as the tops have grown a little, cultivation is started with the horse-hoe and repeated three or four times during the season. On a wet soil, the crop is hilled up, but on sandy soil and very dry soil, level cultivation is given, as hilling up causes the soil to dry up excessively.

The best fertilizer for potatoes is without doubt farm-yard manure, used at the rate of twelve to fifteen tons per acre. But the farmer who grows a large quantity of potatoes is often obliged to use commercial fertilizers. Before purchasing such fertilizers however, he had better make sure that he does not waste any of the plant-food produced on the farm. Too often, a good half of the liquid manure is lost in the stable or outside; this is why the use of cut straw, dried peat, and even saw-dust, as bedding, is strongly urged, in order to absorb the liquid manure which is rich in nitrogen and even in potash, the two most expensive and most important elements in potato growing.

The use of fertilizers alone is not recommended. It is better to use a smaller quantity of farm-yard manure and supplement it with from 75 to 100 pounds of sulphate of potash. The use of nitrate of soda and superphosphate sometimes gives good results on poor lands. The use of complete fertilizers is never advised. Clover ploughed under also gives excellent results.

It is recommended to take the potatoes out of the cellar a few days before planting and put them in a lighted place, not too warm but dry, as this hastens germination. It is better to use potatoes of average size which are cut in three sets or more, each having from two to three good germs. The sets are dusted with plaster and planted as soon as possible.

There is only one insect which attacks the potato crop, viz.: the potato bug or Colorado beetle; it is controlled by Paris green or lead arsenate, or both combined, applied at the right time. It has been observed that the damage caused by this insect is greatly reduced when a regular rotation is practised, that is to say when potatoes are grown only every five of six years on the same soil.

Common scab occurs on lands which are difficult to drain; the use of lime or ashes seems to provoke the growth of this scab.

The most dangerous disease is, without doubt, the powdery scab, which occurs chiefly in farms where potatoes are grown year after year on the same soil; it is not as yet very common. The remedies are the following: Thoroughly disinfect the cellars where the powdery scab has been observed, purchase good tubers for planting, and do not grow potatoes for at least ten years on soils that are known to be infected with the germs of these diseases.

Potatoes keep well in cellars which are well ventilated, dry and dark. When potatoes are piled in heaps several feet deep, slatted ventilators are put through the heaps for the circulation of air. Very good results are also obtained in pits dug in dry soil and lined inside with cedar pieces.

MACDONALD COLLEGE

BY T. G. BUNTING, B.S.A., PROFESSOR OF HORTICULTURE

A considerable quantity of potatoes has been grown at Macdonald College to supply the college demand, amounting to about 2000 bushels per year. These are grown by the Horticultural department on soil varying from sandy loam to clay loam, much of which is not specially adapted to the potato crop. The varieties grown are:—Irish Cobbler, early, and Green Mountain and Gold Coin for main crop. Many other varieties have been tried out but have not proved better, if equal, to the above varieties under our conditions. The Green Mountain and Gold Coin are high class table potatoes when well grown, and they yield well under average good conditions. No definite rotation has been followed here, but during recent years the crop is not grown on the same soil more frequently than once in three years. This is largely on account of the scab, and it has been found that, even with treating the seed potatoes for scab before planting, it is not safe to plant every other year on the same ground.

One of the best rotations that could be followed would be grain, clover and potatoes. By seeding with clover at the time of planting grain a good crop of clover hay should be obtained the second year, and this clover sod should be fall ploughed for potatoes in the third and last year of the rotation. A grass sod, if fall ploughed, should also give good results.

A finer and cleaner crop of potatoes is obtained on the lighter soils and this type of soil is preferred to the moderately heavy clay soils or even clay loam soils. The potato is occasionally used as a cleaning crop to rid the soil of bad weeds and is recommended for this purpose.

Where the field is fall ploughed, particularly a sod field, some preparation is needed in the spring before planting, but when planting from three to five inches deep the preparation of the field is sometimes not completed until after the crop is planted. With very shallow planting one cannot do much harrowing or cultivation until the rows of potatoes are visible, but with deep planting it is possible to cultivate the whole field just as the first plants are coming through, but care must be taken not to disturb the young plants too much or drag them in the soil. Cultivation at this time saves much later work. Three or four cultivations are given to the growing plants, the last one coming just at the blossoming period or a little before and at that time the plants are ridged up two to three inches, just enough to insure that all tubers formed will be covered with soil. We do not get the same results from high ridging of the row, as the plants suffer greatly in a dry season. One hand-hoeing usually suffices but this is dependent on the number of weeds that grow.

We have not been manuring directly for the potato crop, but usually apply manure to the crop preceding the potato and at the time of planting the potato about 600 lb. of fertilizer per acre is used. The composition of this fertilizer varies, depending on the soil, but as most of our soil is not deficient in potash we use a fertilizer fairly high in phosphoric acid, medium in nitrogen and comparatively low in potash.

At times we have been troubled with scab, but where clean seed or moderately clean seed, treated for scab, is used and the potatoes grown on same land but once in three years, we have none. New Brunswick seed gives us good results but is no better than our own seed when it is clean and well grown. We have been seeding at the rate of 15 to 16 bushels per acre.

During the last two seasons we have had practically no late blight, however, we use the Bordeaux mixture (4-4-40) for three sprayings and can usually control the potato beetle with one spraying of arsenate of lead.

The crop is stored in bins in a large root cellar. This cellar is frost proof and comparatively dry, and clean potatoes keep exceptionally well in it.

Very little experimental work is being carried on here in the growing of the potato except in the comparison of the leading varieties and in spraying with the different fungicides and insecticides. No fungicide has been found to replace the Bordeaux mixture, but the dry arsenate of lead is very promising as an insecticide and is a more convenient form than the paste arsenate of lead. The dry arsenate of lead is an acid lead, yet has given no burning on the potato foliage.

ONTARIO

BY PROFESSOR C. A. ZAVITZ, B.S.A., ONTARIO AGRICULTURAL COLLEGE

THE potato (*Solanum tuberosum*), is one of the most important food plants for man. It is easy of propagation, is an abundant yielder, possesses good keeping qualities, and is relished by people generally. The potato is a native of America, and can still be found in the wild state in Chili, and possibly in other countries of South America. In order to distinguish it from the sweet potato it is sometimes called the Irish potato, the English potato, the round potato, or the white potato.

From the report of the Ontario Bureau of Industries for 1913 we learn that for the past thirty-two years the average annual record for the potato crop of Ontario has been 157,765 acres, which yielded 18,292,976 bushels, having a market value of $8,164,660. The average yield of potatoes for Ontario for the thirty-two years from 1882 to 1913 inclusive, has been 116 bushels per acre, and that for the United States for the thirty-four years, from 1880 to 1913 inclusive, has been 83 bushels per acre, or an increase of the former over the latter of practically 71 per cent. The highest average annual yields per acre in the province of Ontario since 1882 were 163 bushels in 1884, and 159 bushels in 1895 and in 1914; and in the United States since 1880 were 113.4 bushels in 1912, 110.4 bushels in 1903, 106.8 bushels in 1909, 102.2 bushels in 1906, and 101 bushels in 1905. In all of the other years the average yield in the United States was less than 100 bushels per acre per annum. The lowest annual average yield per acre in Ontario was 76.1 bushels in 1887, and in the United States 56 bushels in 1890.

According to the Census and Statistics Monthly for Canada the annual average market value of the potatoes produced in the Dominion amounted to $35,985,000, and in Ontario to $11,486,000. According to the same source of information Ontario has produced 32 per cent, Quebec, 23 per cent, and New Brunswick, 10 per cent of the market value of the average annual potato crop of the Dominion for the past five years.

Not only has the average yield of potatoes in Ontario varied greatly in different seasons but it has also varied in the different localities throughout the province. Usually the highest average yields have been produced in the northern and eastern, and the lowest average yields in the south-western portions of Ontario. As the average yield of potatoes per acre in Wellington county, in which the Agricultural College is located, has been very similar to the average yield throughout the province for the past thirty-three years the results of experiments conducted at Guelph should form a good general guide for Ontario.

VARIETIES OF POTATOES

We have had under experiment at the Ontario Agricultural College upwards of three hundred varieties of potatoes. It is the policy to test all varieties for at least five years, after which the most desirable kinds are continued in the experiments, and the others are dropped from the list.

Early Varieties:—As there is usually much interest taken in early potatoes it was thought advisable to make a special test of some of the early kinds. Only a few of the varieties which had been grown in the general experiment were selected for the test. The experiment was conducted for six years in succession by planting four rows of each variety in the spring, and digging two rows of each at the end of nine weeks, and two rows of each at the end of twelve weeks after the seed was planted, in order to ascertain which variety of potatoes would give the best results in the shortest possible time after planting. The experiment was conducted in duplicate. The following table gives the average results of the twelve tests conducted during the six year period, in bushels of potatoes per acre per annum:—

RESULTS OF SIX YEARS' EXPE IMENTS WITH EARLY POTATOES.

Varieties of Early Potatoes	Nine Weeks	Twelve Weeks
Early Andes	159.6	251.5
Six Weeks	156.5	245.2
Early Fortune	153.8	230.8
Early Dominion	152.9	255.7
Early Dawn	151.7	239.6
Early Pinkeye	145.9	240.3
Early Ohio	142.9	227.6
Stray Beauty	111.7	197.9
Burpee's Extra Early	104.7	225.4

but the results were reversed three weeks later.

Since this experiment was concluded other varieties have been added to the general potato experiment. The following gives the average yield of potatoes per acre per annum of each of four varieties for four years: Extra Early Eureka, 208.4 bushels; Irish Cobbler, 191.5 bushels; Early Fortune, 187.8 bushels, and Early Ohio, 163.4 bushels. The Extra Early Eureka and the Irish Cobbler resemble each other in appearance, but the former has surpassed the latter in productiveness. The Irish Cobbler variety of potatoes has been increased largely throughout Ontario in recent years. The two varieties of early potatoes which are probably grown the most extensively throughout the province at present are the Irish Cobbler and the Early Ohio.

EXPERIMENTAL PLOTS WITH POTATOES BEING PLANTED WITH GREAT CARE ON THE COLLEGE FARM AT GUELPH.

These results show that there was a marked difference in the yields of each variety from the two dates of digging. This, however, was more marked in some cases than in others; as for instance, the Stray Beauty gave a larger yield of potatoes per acre than the Burpee's Extra Early at the end of the nine week period,

Late Varieties:—Each of four varieties of late potatoes have been under experiment at the Ontario Agricultural College for the past twenty-five years without change of seed from an outside source. It is interesting to note that during the past ten years fully one-half the yields have been higher than those for the average of the whole period of twenty-five years. In the case of two of the varieties the highest yields were produced in the twenty-third year in which the potatoes had been grown on the College farm. The following gives the average yield per annum, in bushels per acre, of each of the four varieties for the twenty-five year period:—

	Bushels.
Empire State	219.9
Rose's New Invincible	216.2
Rural New Yorker, No. 2	208.4
White Elephant	198.7

The Empire State has proven to be not only a high yielder, but the potatoes are of excellent quality.

the unfavourable weather conditions for the production of a late potato of the highest quality.

In 1914 an enquiry was made throughout Ontario regarding the most extensively grown varieties of potatoes in the various counties of the Province. In all fifty-one varieties were mentioned one or more times as being the most extensively grown in the different counties. As a result of a similar enquiry fifty-seven varieties were mentioned in 1913, and fifty-eight varieties in 1912. It is to be hoped that the number of varieties is gradually decreasing in the Province, and that within a

IN THE FOREGROUND WILL BE SEEN A FEW OF THE MANY EXPERIMENTS WITH POTATOES IN THE TRIAL GROUNDS AT THE ONTARIO AGRICULTURAL COLLEGE.

During the past eight years the highest yielding variety of potatoes has been the Davies' Warrior. This variety was imported from southern Scotland about ten years ago. The average yield per acre per annum of the Davies' Warrior for the past eight years has been 252.2 bushels, and of the Empire State for the same period, 192.4 bushels. The Davies' Warrior is a white potato of good quality. As it is a late potato, however, it has not done quite as well in each of the past two years as it did formerly. This is probably owing to

comparatively short time the farmers will confine themselves largely to a few of the highest yielding varieties of the best quality. The following gives the names, and the order of the varieties which were mentioned the greatest number of times in 1914: Rural New Yorker No. 2, 32; Delaware, 25; Carman, 19; Empire State and Irish Cobbler, each 16; Early Rose, 14; White Elephant, 13; Extra Early Eureka, 9; American Wonder, 8; and Green Mountain, 7. If we take into consideration the answers to enquiries in each of the past eight years we find that the Rural New Yorker No. 2 has been grown more extensively than any other variety, and this has been followed by the Empire State as the second most extensively grown variety.

SOIL CONDITIONS

Potatoes are grown on a great variety of soils throughout Ontario, but they do particularly well and are grown extensively for commercial purposes in sections where there is a fertile sandy loam.

Place in the Rotation.—The position of the potato crop in the rotation is not uniform throughout Ontario. It is probably safe to say, however, that the potatoes are grown after clover and grass more frequently than after any other crop. They require a considerable amount of vegetable matter in the soil, and the clover sod leaves the land in a friable open condition which is particularly suitable for potato growing.

Preparation.—Sod land is generally ploughed deeply in the autumn and allowed to remain uncultivated for the winter. In the spring it is usually left undisturbed, or probably harrowed once or twice previous to the preparation of the seed bed for the potato crop. Planting takes place on the average about the twentieth of May although in some sections the planting does not take place until two or three weeks later. The early varieties are frequently planted near the beginning of the month of May, especially if they are grown to supply the first market. Some farmers instead of ploughing the land in the autumn do not plough the sod until time for planting the potatoes when they drop the tubers in every third furrow. Although this method is not as reliable, satisfactory results are frequently obtained if the weather conditions are favourable.

Cultivation.—It is usually a good plan to harrow the land soon after the potatoes are planted and before the tops have appeared above the ground. The land can usually be harrowed once or twice after the potato tops have made their appearance. For best results the crop should be cultivated every week or ten days if the weather is comparatively dry. It is a good plan to cultivate the potatoes as soon as the land is in proper condition after each heavy rain. This tends to conserve moisture, liberate plant food, keep the potatoes free from weeds, and stimulate rapid growth. Experiments were conducted at Guelph in each of ten years in which level and hilled cultivation were compared. In the dry years the level cultivation gave the highest returns, and in those seasons in which there was a considerable amount of rain fall the hilled land produced the heaviest crops. In the average of the ten years' experiments there was practically no difference in yield per acre from the two systems of cultivation. It is probably an advantage, however, to slightly elevate the soil along the rows of the potatoes, especially during the last cultivations.

FERTILIZATION

As a result of experiments conducted at the Ontario Agricultural College in each of five years it was found that the Royal Canadian and the Potato fertilizer gave the highest yields of potatoes per acre of the different commercial fertilizers used in the five years' experiment. In another experiment, extending over a period of five years, in which several fertilizers were used, the highest yield per acre was obtained from a mixed fertilizer similar to the one used in our co-operative experiments, and which was composed of nitrate of soda, muriate of potash and superphosphate in the proportion by weight of 1, 1 and 2, and which was applied at the rate of 213 pounds per acre. This was followed by the Royal Canadian and the Potato fertilizer, each of which was applied at the rate of 320 pounds per acre. Based on these and other results, a co-operative experiment was conducted in each of five years previous to 1912, in which six different fertilizers were compared with each other, with farmyard manure, and with no fertilizer with potatoes. The average results of this experiment conducted within the five year period on 98 farms of Ontario were reported in 1911. The average results of the 98 experiments showed the yield of potatoes per acre to be as follows: Unfertilized land, 129.2 bushels; 160 pounds of nitrate of soda, 133.4 bushels; 160 pounds of muriate of potash, 160.8 bushels; 320 pounds of superphosphate, 156.8 bushels; 213 pounds of the complete fertilizer previously described, 166.8 bushels; 320 pounds of potato fertilizer, 167.5 bushels; 320 pounds of Royal Canadian fertilizer, 164.5 bushels; and twenty tons of cow manure, 174.7 bushels. According to the prices given for the manure and the fertilizers in 1911, the increased yield of potatoes was produced at a cost per bushel for the complete fertilizer of 11.3 cents; muriate of potash, 12.7 cents; cow manure, 13.2 cents; superphosphate, 14.2 cents; potato fertilizer, 14.4 cents; Royal Canadian fertilizer, 15.9 cents, and nitrate of soda, 19.8 cents.

Based on the results of past experiments it was thought wise to start a co-operative experiment in testing different quantities of fertilizers per acre in comparison with each other, with farmyard manure alone, with farmyard manure and fertilizer, and with unfertilized land. We, therefore, placed on our list an experiment with fertilizers, cow manure, and no fertilizer with potatoes, in the spring of 1912, and we conducted experiments in 120 places throughout the province in each of the past three years. In each of these years we divided the number into four groups of thirty each, and used the Royal Canadian fertilizer for one group, the potato fertilizer for another, a fertilizer composed of nitrate of soda, muriate of potash, and superphosphate, in the proportion by weight of 7, 9, and 16, for another, and a fertilizer composed of nitrate of soda, muriate of potash and superphosphate, in the proportion of 1, 1 and 2 for the fourth group. Each of the first three fertilizers were applied alone at the rate of 320, 640, and 960 pounds per acre, and 320 pounds in combination with ten tons of cow manure per acre. In comparison with these, another plot received cow manure at the rate of twenty tons per acre, and one plot was left unfertilized. For No. 4 group the fertilizer was used in the same proportion, with the exception that the minimum amount was 213 instead of 320 pounds per acre. Owing to the unusual weather conditions in 1912 the potato rot was very prevalent and many of the results of the fertilizer experiments obtained could not be used on that account. There were, however, nineteen good reports of successfully conducted experiments with fertilizers and potatoes obtained in which the rot did not prove troublesome and which represented fairly well the four different kinds of fertilizers distributed. In 1913 we received in all thirty-one good reports, there being from six to ten good reports for each group. In 1914 twenty-eight good reports of successfully conducted experiments were received, there being exactly seven good reports for each separate test. We therefore have for the three years seventy-eight good reports three years seventy-eight good reports of successfully conducted experiments. The following table gives the average results of the fifty-eight reports of the successfully conducted experiments of the first three groups in the past three years, and also the average results of twenty tests made in the last three years with fertilizers of group 4:—

RESULTS OF CO-OPERATIVE FERTILIZER EXPERIMENTS.

Fertilizers and Manure.	Quantity per Acre. Pounds.	Yield of Potatoes per Acre. (bus.)	
		Groups 1, 2 and 3. Average 3 years. 3 sets. 58 tests.	Group 4. Average 3 years. 20 tests.
1. No Fertilizer	...	128.3	142.3
2. Fertilizer	320	150.1	165.9
3. Fertilizer	640	161.2	180.4
4. Fertilizer	960	175.0	190.4
5. Fertilizer	320 }		
6. Cow Manure	20,000 } (10 tons)	175.1	194.1
Cow Manure	40,000 (20 tons)	177.6	194.3

The fertilizers used for groups 1, 2 and 3 were somewhat similar in composition, all containing nitrogen, potash and phosphoric acid. The results as here presented are those from general fertilizers used in different quantities on what might be termed the average soil of Ontario, as the experiments were conducted on 58 different farms. It will be seen that on the average there was an increase in the yield of potatoes per acre of 21.8 bushels from 320 pounds of fertilizer; 32.9 bushels from 640 pounds of fertilizer; and 46.7 bushels from 960 pounds of fertilizer. The yield per acre increased as the amount of fertilizer used became greater. From a study of these results it would seem as though the first 320 pounds of fertilizer increased the yield 21.8 bushels; the second 320 pounds, 11.1 bushels; and the third 320 pounds, 13.8 bushels. It will also be observed that the 20 tons of cow manure per acre increased the yield of potatoes 49.3 bushels or 2.5 bushels per acre more than the combination of 10 tons of cow manure and 320 pounds of fertilizer per acre. The average results of the twenty tests in group 4 are fairly similar to those of the other three groups already discussed. The amount of fertilizer for plot 2 in group 4 consisted of 213 instead of 320 pounds per acre and is identical with the complete fertilizer used for five years throughout Ontario in experiments conducted on 98 farms previously referred to. From a study of the results in the foregoing table the increases in the yields of potatoes which were made at the lowest cost in the average results for the three years were obtained from 320 pounds of complete fertilizer as represented by groups 1, 2 and 3, and from 213 pounds of the fertilizer composed of nitrate of soda, muriate of potash, and superphosphate, in the proportion by weight of 1, 1 and 2. In the last result referred to there was an increase of 23.6 bushels per acre produced at a cost of approximately $4.24 for the fertilizer which would be about 18 cents for each bushel of increase in the potato crop.

Fertilizers are not used very extensively throughout Ontario. Their use is apparently increasing, however, on such crops as potatoes, mangels, sugar beets, and fruit. The fertilizers can be used more economically with potatoes than with the grain crops.

DISEASES

There are a few diseases which affect the potato crop of Ontario. Much caution, however, has been exercised in keeping such diseases as the potato canker and the

Powdery Scab from being introduced into the province. A few of the other diseases are effectually treated by our most progressive potato growers.

Treatment for Potato Scab.—Experiments have been conducted at the college in using different treatments for the potato scab. One of the best methods adopted has been the formalin treatment. This consists in treating the scabby potatoes by soaking them for two hours in a solution of formalin made by mixing one pint of the forty per cent formaldehyde with thirty gallons of water. This amount is sufficient for treating fifteen or twenty bushels of potatoes.

Treatment for Blight.—Various methods have been used for the treatment for blight. One of the most effectual of these has been the use of the Bordeaux mixture with a machine which is so constructed as to spray both the upper and the lower parts of the leaves. Three treatments conducted in this way have been more effectual than five or six treatments where the vines were sprayed simply on the upper surface.

CONCLUSION

One of the weaknesses in connection with potato growing in Ontario has been the lack of co-operation in the production of the best varieties, and the proper delivery of the potatoes in the best markets. This weakness, however, is being remedied by the formation of Co-operative Societies such as the one in the Rainy River District, the one at Caledon in Halton County, etc. Separate varieties particularly suited to the locality are used, as for instance, the Extra Early Eureka variety in the Rainy River District, and the Dooley variety in Caradoc, Middlesex County. With the proper establishment of Co-operative Societies in the potato growing districts of Ontario there is no reason why we cannot produce in this province an increasing quantity of potatoes of superior quality. If all the farmers of Ontario would confine their attention to two or three of the best early, and two or three of the best late varieties of potatoes, there would be a higher production, the potato crop would be of better quality, and the prices realized would be higher than those secured at the present time. There will probably be marked improvements in potato production in Ontario in the near future.

MANITOBA

BY S. A. BEDFORD, DEPUTY MINISTER OF AGRICULTURE

THE Manitoba Department of Agriculture has found that for early crop the best varieties of potatoes are the Early Bovee and the Early Ohio; for general crop the Carman, Late Puritan, Manitoba Wonder and Wee MacGregor varieties.

Potatoes in Manitoba are generally raised in a separate plot devoted to vegetables and are not reckoned in crop rotation. The soil is prepared for potatoes by deep plowing in the spring or fall; before planting the land is harrowed, then rolled; the potatoes are planted in every third furrow, making the rows three feet apart; the seed is deposited, nine inches apart in the row, at a depth of from three to three-and-one-half inches. The best results have been obtained from selecting fair-sized tubers typical of the variety and by cutting to three-eye sets. The cultivation requirements are to harrow directly after planting and thereafter every few days until the tops are four inches or five inches high; the plot is then cultivated with a one or two horse machine between the rows until blossom appears, when the rows are slightly hilled to prevent exposure of the tubers.

From 10 to 15 tons of well rotted barnyard manure is used per acre for fertilization purposes. No commercial fertilizers are used.

The seed being healthy generally in Manitoba, it is not necessary to treat it; but sometimes a treatment with formalin would improve scabby seed. Neither is the growing crop treated for diseases as a rule; but it

In connection with the marketing of potato crops very little has been done in Manitoba; but the Department is encouraging the production of larger crops of improved varieties by the publication of bulletins on gardening and by holding meetings in districts where potatoes and other truck crops are largely grown.

We find that the quality of potatoes depends very largely upon the character of the soil. It is exceedingly difficult to get a potato of high

VEGETABLES GROWN AT DAUPHIN, MAN.
This Exhibit won over 62 First Prizes and 21 Second Prizes.

is generally found necessary to use Paris green for Colorado beetle.

The crop is stored in the basements of large buildings in the cities and keeps very well there when properly ventilated. Farmers usually store in the house cellars, which are sometimes much too warm for the best results. We find that it is very important to have the seed tubers carefully stored in a cool temperature during the winter months as badly sprouted potatoes lack vigour.

quality from the rich, black clay loam such as we have in the Red River Valley; the tuber absorbs too much moisture for the best results. Sandy loams, however,—and these are the general rule outside of the Red River Valley—give a potato of high quality and, if properly treated, excellent yields.

The growing of potatoes is an important feature of the Manitoba Boys' and Girls' Clubs and splendid results are being obtained.

SASKATCHEWAN

BY J. BRACKEN, B.S.A., PROFESSOR OF FIELD HUSBANDRY, UNIVERSITY OF SASKATCHEWAN

THE earliest varieties of potatoes we have grown here are Early Andes, Early Triumph, and Early Ohio. Early Ohio is a little later than either of the other two, but is a much heavier yielder. We look upon this as a leading early sort for this district.

Everett and Irish Cobbler are leading medium early sorts. The former is a little heavier in yield than the latter but is pink in colour, while Irish Cobbler is white.

Several of the late sorts have done exceedingly well with us. Table Talk, Carman No. 3, Gold Coin, and Wee McGregor are among those we look upon with greatest favour.

In Saskatchewan the potato crop should generally be planted on fallowed land, for two reasons: (1) because the yield is greater than on soil prepared in any other way; and, (2) the crop following potatoes planted on fallowed land can be counted on to produce satisfactorily. For potatoes, the fallow should be ploughed deeply as early as possible in the month of June, and the surface of the field cultivated sufficiently thereafter to keep down weed growth and to maintain a mulch. On land prepared in this way the seed may be ploughed in to a depth of four or five inches, with every prospect of good returns. If the seed is dropped and covered, the land should be packed and harrowed; another harrowing at the time the plants are showing themselves above ground is generally advisable, and additional harrowing should be given when necessary to control the growth of small annual weeds, and to maintain a surface mulch. Thorough inter-tillage thereafter is essential.

In 1914 potatoes cultivated four times produced nineteen bushels more total yield per acre than the same variety on the same land cultivated twice.

"Hilling" is not so necessary under average soil conditions in this province as in more humid regions. Our results to date seem to indicate that throwing the earth up around the plants to a medium height is to be preferred over a higher hilling.

As yet we have no data on the value of fertilizers of any kind on the potato crop, either under garden or field conditions. From this time forward, however, we shall have data on the effect of each of twenty-one different combinations of fertilizers on the potato crop.

All our seed is treated every spring with formalin. Last year, experiments were started to test the relative value of formalin and corrosive sublimate on the yield and control of disease in potatoes. No blight has yet been observed in our potato crop, so that opportunity for studying the control of this disease has not presented itself.

Our crop is stored in a basement cellar, the temperature of which we aim to keep between 33 degrees F. and 40 degrees F. The potatoes lose less weight at the lower temperature and develop rather less decay.

Much additional work is under way now. The crop management practices such as dates of planting and rates of planting, distance apart of plants in the row and size of seed, have been under observation for two years.

In 1914 the earliest planting (April 30th), produced the largest return. This, however, is rather too early for planting the main crop. Two ounce sets from medium or large seed seems thus far to result in greater productiveness than the use of smaller sets or from the same size sets from smaller seed. It is our opinion that smaller sets may with profit be planted when the soil and climatic conditions are all favourable. Sufficient data is not at present at hand to determine positively the best distance between the rows, or the best distance between plants within the row. Our present policy, however, is to plant the potatoes in rows thirty-two inches apart, and from twelve to sixteen inches apart in the row. This practice, as pointed out, is more or less arbitrary.

During the past four years our yields have varied from approximately 100 bushels per acre in the dry year of 1914 to nearly 600 bushels per acre in the moist year of 1911, these yields in both cases coming from our fallowed land.

ALBERTA

BY GEO. HARCOURT, B.S.A., DEPUTY MINISTER OF AGRICULTURE

EXCEPT in a few districts potatoes have not been looked upon as an important crop, i.e., a money crop, with the result that little attention has been paid to early planting and suitable varieties. Any time after seeding, too frequently, is considered good enough to plant. The result is that owing to the short growing season an early fall frost is liable to check growth and give an unripened yield. Late maturing varieties have been planted, frequently with the same result.

VARIETIES

So far as can be ascertained the following varieties are suitable for early cropping in the order named:— Irish Cobbler, Rochester Rose, Early Bovee, Early Ohio and Vick's Extra Early.

For a general crop:—Wee Mac-Gregor, Gold Coin, Table Talk, American Wonder, Country Gentleman, Holborn's Abundance, Early Moonlight, Sutton's Satisfaction and Burbank.

Farmers, generally, are growing too many varieties, but owing to the fact that Alberta possesses more hill and dale, more diversified conditions because of its nearness to the Rocky Mountains, the question of suitableness of variety is a big problem and every man is trying to work it out for himself. Such experimentations, however, inevitably lead to difficulty in marketing, because of the inability to secure carloads of any one variety. The market here prefers white-skinned potatoes, medium in size and with small or shallow eyes.

SOIL

Owing to the large amount of decayed vegetation in the soil much of the land in the province is not as suitable for growing potatoes as could be desired. Here, as elsewhere, a fairly sandy soil, well drained, gives best results.

So far but little attention has been paid to growing potatoes for market, hence no definite place in a rotation or plan of cropping has been chosen for potatoes. On irrigated land in the southern portion of the province potatoes have given phenomenal yields on well worked alfalfa sod. In the south also a well worked summer fallow presents the ideal place for potatoes and the cultivation puts the land in excellent shape for wheat. Farther north good results usually follow on well worked timothy sod. As potatoes make a light draft on the moisture of the soil there is no reason why they should not be planted in soil that is to be summer fallowed. The cultivation given will put the land in as good condition for a wheat crop as a summer fallow.

Stubble land should be ploughed in the fall, packed in areas where the rainfall is limited and disced to put in shape to retain moisture and pass the winter. It should be worked at intervals in the spring to kill weeds, conserve moisture and warm the land.

Flat cultivation is best in areas of limited rainfall. A certain amount of hilling may be necessary but unnecessary hilling means loss of moisture. Harrowing should begin as soon as the potatoes are planted and continued at intervals until the potatoes are well through the ground. Cultivation between the rows should then be continued to preserve moisture and kill weeds. If the early harrowing is well done there should be little need of any hoeing.

MANURING

Owing to the soil being new, practically no commercial fertilizers are used. They have been tried but the increased yield has not been sufficient to warrant the expense. Where manure has been used, well rotted barnyard manure has given the best results. It should be applied the previous year and well worked into the soil.

DISEASES

So far Alberta has been fairly free from any trouble with potato diseases. Scab is the most prevalent and is always worse where fresh barnyard manure is used. Treatment of the seed with formalin will give good results in eradicating scab and bi-chloride of mercury where blight has been noticed. Ravages by insect pests are nil; the potato bug not having found its way here in sufficient numbers as yet.

STORAGE

The inclination on the part of the farmer is to sell his crop out of the field and not to hold for a rise in the market in the spring. The more progressive farmers are beginning to build storage cellars or root houses, the more simple of these being excavations in a side hill, shored up with poles and covered with three alternate layers of straw and earth, with ventilation stacks.

The Department, realizing that farmers were growing too many varieties and that there were districts where the soil was highly suited to growing potatoes of a high quality, endeavoured to bring about improved conditions by starting co-operative experiments under the supervision of the *Vermilion School of Agriculture, the Provincial Demonstration Farm and the local agricultural societies at Vermilion and Stony Plain. The result at Stony Plain last year, where six different varieties were tried out on six different farms, has resulted in the creation of such interest that two varieties only will be planted this spring by a large number of the members of the societies. It is hoped that in this way it will be possible to market many carloads of uniform potatoes next fall. The society is arranging for a supply of seed.

Once definite results are obtained, this work will likely be extended to other districts. The province can grow good potatoes, if the right seed, care and attention are given.

*See AGRICULTURAL GAZETTE, January, 1915, p. 77.

BRITISH COLUMBIA
BY W. NEWTON, ASSISTANT SOIL AND CROP INSPECTOR

THE total potato production in British Columbia has steadily increased. Recognition of the high quality of potatoes from many districts is doing much to establish the potato as a staple money crop in the province.

FIELD CROP COMPETITIONS

The field crop competitions in potatoes has become an important phase of the work of the Department of Agriculture. Last year forty-two competitions in potatoes were conducted through the Farmers' Institutes. The announcement of this competition was published in a bulletin form containing a brief description of the most approved cultural methods, and copies were distributed to all members of Farmers' Institutes. This competition had in most cases the desired results. The competitive spirit led large numbers of farmers to handle their potato crop along approved lines. Many valuable demonstrations resulted, the more noticeable of which were fertilizing tests and the value of Bordeaux mixture as a spray. In many cases good results were also reported in using the "formalin solution" as a preventative for scab. The minimum size of a plot entered in the competition was one half acre. Awards were based on a field score.

A bonus is offered this year to any competitor who will send in a satisfactory statement of the cost of production of the crop entered. We feel that this will give the department valuable data as to which districts are suitable to profitable potato growing. The main object, however, is to encourage the farmers to keep crop records. In order to obtain uniform statements, forms are being supplied and the competitors are requested to fill in the data asked for.

BOYS AND GIRLS' COMPETITIONS

Apart from the regular competition in potatoes, twenty Farmers' Institutes held Boys and Girls' Competitions. These were conducted along much the same lines as the above. The size of the plot had to be exactly 1/10 acre. The awards in this competition were based on three scores, a field score, a score on a harvested exhibit of twenty pounds and a certified report score. The score cards were contained in the announcement of the competition and were made as educational as possible. This was especially true of the certified reports. On this report a list of questions was asked, to bring to the attention of each boy or girl every step that experienced growers take to ensure a good potato crop. In the same report questions as to expenditures and receipts drew to the children's attention the value of keeping records.

A stipulation worthy of note in this junior competition was that all competitors within an "Institute District" had to use the same variety. We feel that the large number of varieties in this province if reduced to a limited number of standard varieties adapted to the districts would materially assist in marketing, especially in the districts getting into the car-shipping class.

VARIETIES

We do not feel we are yet in a position to name the varieties that are best adapted to different districts. Carman No. 1, and Burbank have done well, Carman No. 1 on lighter soils and Burbank on heavier. The order of popularity in the crop competitions is an indication as to their merits. The order is as follows: Carman No. 1, Burbank, Gold Coin, Early Rose, Up to Date, Wee Mac-

Gregor and Money Maker. The three first are outstanding in popularity.

Copies of all field crop scores are kept on file and the Department has made use of them in recommending to persons desiring good seed those growers whose scores were outstanding.

POTATO CENTRES

Arrangements have been made for this season to introduce a good strain of Carman No. 1 to districts around Armstrong, Grand Forks and Kamloops. A field selection will be made during the coming season and will be continued from year to year under our supervision. The object of this selection is to produce a supply of "Elite Stock Seed" for growers in the district. The growers will be enlisted in the Canadian Seed Growers Association and will be ultimately organized into a "Potato Centre."

FERTILIZER EXPERIMENT

The following fertilizer experiment was carried out at Errington under our supervision during 1914 on newly cleared land. The plot was drained with 6 inch tile 60 feet apart. Inasmuch as it was the first year under cultivation the land was not in good tilth. The soil was a sandy loam resting on a sandy clay sub-soil.

Plot No.	Area.	Treatment		Yield.
1	⅛ acre.	100 lb.	Nitrate of Soda	70 lb.
2	⅛ acre.	233 lb.	Superphosphates of Lime	40 "
3	⅛ acre.	100 lb.	Muriate of Potash	110 "
4	⅛ acre.	{ 600 lb.	Nitrate of Soda	
		140 lb.	Superphosphate of Lime	70 "
5			Check Block	30 "
6		75 lb.	Nitrate of Soda	
		75 lb.	Muriate of Potash	100 "
7	⅛ acre.	235 lb.	of "A" Fertilizer	110 "
8		700 lb.	Lime	20 "
9	⅛ acre.	60 lb.	Muriate of Potash	110 "
10	⅛ acre.	Stable Manure		100 "

SPRAYING EXPERIMENTS (1914)

Four 1½ acre plots, one at Hammond, two at Chilliwack and one at Ladner were treated as follows:—½ acre sprayed five times; ½ acre sprayed three times; and ½ acre not sprayed, used for a check plot. The following is a summary of the results:

RESULTS OF SPRAYING EXPERIMENT

	Sprayed. 5-times.	Sprayed. 3-times.	Check. Not sprayed.
Hammond	3.65 tons.	3.6	3.32 tons.
Chilliwack	3.25 tons.	4 tons.	3.1
Marketable discarded	.31	.26	.31
Ladner marketable	5.85	5.6	4.1
Discarded	1.0	1.05	2.7

Bordeaux (4-4-40) was used as the sprays. The past season being unusually dry the late blight was not so prevalent. We therefore feel that the continuation of this experiment will secure valuable data as to the amount of spraying that is profitable.

STORING

The storage problem in British Columbia has not met with any serious difficulty. A cool, well-ventilated cellar or root-house which is perfectly dark is recommended. Too much stress cannot be put on good ventilation. If there is not a good system of ventilation, slats can be nailed a little apart about 5 or 6 inches from the wall. A false floor with cracks between the boards can be put 6 inches above the permanent floor. This allows the air to circulate around and through the pile. If the pile is very large, slatted ventilators can be placed here and there from top to bottom. The temperature should be as low as possible without freezing, and at the same time the air should be as dry as possible.

In the dryer sections of British Columbia, the potatoes are often pitted. The pit that is recommended is 6 to 8 feet wide, about 8 inches deep and as long as needed. The potatoes are placed in the pit about 4 feet deep and covered with enough straw to keep the earth from coming through, and then about 1 foot of earth is placed on top of this.

A strip along the top is left uncovered for a week or two for ventilation. If there is danger of rain, this can be covered with sacking. When this strip is covered a small hole for ventilation is left every 8 or 10 feet. If in the winter time there is danger of freezing, the pit can be covered with some strawy manure, and the ventilation holes filled in.

MARKETING

The tendency of the crop competitions is to establish a standard variety in each district. This work coupled with the establishment of organized potato-growing "centres" we believe to be the foundation to successful co-operative marketing.

The importance of all phases of potato production is fully realized, and every effort to stimulate the production of this important food product will be made in British Columbia.

The first distribution of seed by the Department of Agriculture of British Columbia was to Kamloops: 1,200 bushels of wheat and 1,800 bushels of oats; to Vernon: 1,200 bushels of wheat and 1,800 bushels of oats; to Vancouver: 1,200 bushels of wheat and 1,800 bushels of oats, and to Nelson 150 bushels of wheat and 1,200 bushels of oats. The charge is 3 cents a pound for each variety of seed.

The outlook for live stock in British Columbia, according to Live Stock Commissioner, W. T. McDonald, of British Columbia, is exceptionally satisfactory. There is much activity both in the dairy and meat business, particularly along the line of the Grand Trunk Pacific and in the Nechaco and Bulkley valleys. Several large dairies have been opened in the fruit-growing section of Okanagan. The number of sheep is increasing. The milk tests being carried on by the Department of Agriculture are proving most beneficial.

QUEBEC

AGRICULTURAL LEGISLATION

A T the session for 1915 of the Quebec Legislature, recently brought to a conclusion, several bills relating to agricultural societies were passed, as well as a measure authorizing municipalities to make advances for the purchase of seed.

The Act relating to co-operative agricultural societies of 1909 was amended to give associations or directorates power to decide on the day for inspection, providing one such day be set per month.

The Act relating to the Provincial Dairy Association and to the manufacture of dairy products was amended to include two new paragraphs, the first defining the composition of the Association and the second authorizing it to divide the province into regions under approval by the Lieutenant-Governor in Council.

Provision is also made for the appointment of inspectors-general and assistant inspectors-general by the Lieutenant-Governor in Council, their duties being to superintend the production and supply of milk as well as the manufacture of butter and cheese. Other clauses relate to the election of directors, to the rules and regulations and to the advertising of meetings. A further provision calls for the appointment at every factory of a head butter maker, who shall be properly certificated. By-laws adopted by co-operative agricultural societies, relating to butter and cheese, cream and milk, must be approved by the Inspector-General. Societies can recover damages if supplied with unwholesome or sour milk. Sterilization is made compulsory. Reports of the operations of each factory must be made to the Minister of Agriculture on or before January 15th in each year.

Another Act requires the manager of every co-operative agricultural society to make a report in triplicate of the state of affairs and to file one copy with the provincial secretary and another with the clerk or secretary-treasurer of the municipality.

Council-Bill No. 109 is the Act relating to the aid that may be granted by municipalities for the purchase of seed grain and seeds during the year 1915. This measure authorizes the council of any rural municipality or any county council governing a territory not erected into a local municipality to take out of the funds of the municipality, or borrow, the sums necessary to fulfil the object of the Act, terms of repayment of the loans that can only be made to ratepayers to be fixed by the council.

AGRICULTURAL APPROPRIATIONS
1915-1916

Agricultural Societies	$145,000
Agricultural Circles, encouragement of agriculture in general, including subsidy to South Shore Railway Company	110,000
The Agricultural and Horticultural Society of Montreal	500
Pomological and Fruit Growing Society of the Province of Quebec	500
Horticultural Society, Quebec	500
Council of Agriculture	3,000
Agricultural Schools	30,000
Veterinary Instruction	5,500
Domestic Science Schools	16,000
Dairy Society of the Province of Quebec	2,000
Dairy School of St. Hyacinthe, and working of farm	8,000
Grants to Butter and Cheese Syndicates, and Inspection of same	28,000
Towards the encouragement of the Dairy Industry generally	32,000
Encouragement of the cultivation of fruit trees, (Horticulture)	10,000
Official Laboratory of the Province of Quebec	2,000
Lectures on Agriculture	9,000
Journal of Agriculture	30,000
Encouragement to Poultry Raising	3,000
Provincial Agricultural Merit	3,500
Arbor Day	100
Exhibitions	32,000
Total	$470,600

MAPLE SUGAR INDUSTRY

BY J. ANTONIO GRENIER, B.A., SECRETARY, DEPARTMENT OF AGRICULTURE

JUDGING by present appearances, we will have an early spring this year. A number of maple bushes are already reported to be tapped in Eastern townships. Therefore the three sugar-making schools of the Department of Agriculture will soon be open; considerable improvements were made in these schools during the summer with a view to increase their efficiency. Requests for admission from farmers or farmers' sons are received daily, and we expect to have a large attendance during the next sugaring season.

In order to reach a large number of our farmers, a number of articles on sugar making were printed this spring in the JOURNAL OF AGRICULTURE and a circular giving practical hints, easy to follow, was distributed.

It is the intention of the Minister to have practical demonstrations given by an expert in some of the sugar houses of the province, and particularly in the counties of Portneuf and Champlain which are remote from the sugar-making schools. One of our lecturers who is attending short courses that are now being given in the various agricultural centres along the lines of the Canadian Northern and the Canadian Pacific railways between Quebec and Montreal, has already visited some sugar houses in order to encourage the farmers to improve their material and their methods.

The convention of the Pure Maple Sugar and Syrup Farmers' Co-operative Association was held last summer in the county of Beauce which is well known for its large number of sugar plants. The lectures that were given at the convention and the work of our sugar-making school at Beauceville will help to improve the quality of the products.

This association has made arrangements with the Quebec Cheesemakers' Agricultural Co-operative Association, who have warehouses in Montreal, for the sale of the sugar and syrup manufactured by its members. The chief co-operative associations of the province have also been invited to send their products which will be graded by an employee of the Department of Agriculture and sold according to the quality, as is already done for butter, cheese, eggs, poultry and cured meats. These courses which are given in the schools for the maple-bush owners; the demonstrations; the lectures; the associations through which the products are sold according to their quantity and not at a price arbitrarily set by the trade; the new law of adulteration which protects the producers as well as the consumers; the utilisation of the very profitable by-products; all these factors will surely give a new life to this splendid industry of maple products which is, we might say, a specialty of our province, and they afford the hope that the production will double in a few years.

NOTE:—This article was written by Mr. Grenier, on March 17, 1915.

The man that can see no patriotism in production when the Empire is struggling for existence is himself most in need of patriotic stimulation.—*C. C. James.*

ONTARIO

DEMONSTRATION LECTURES FOR WOMEN'S INSTITUTES

BY GEO. A. PUTNAM, B.S.A., DEPARTMENT OF AGRICULTURE, TORONTO, ONT.

THE enthusiastic interest which the Women's Institutes have taken in the itinerary Demonstration-Lecture courses in "Food Values and Cooking," "Sewing", and "Home Nursing" provided by the Ontario Department of Agriculture for the past three years, led to a new experiment this year. Instead of holding a class at five different points in a district each week for ten weeks, a teacher was sent to give a two to four weeks' course at one central point, the lessons to be free to any woman or girl in the district, whether, an Institute member or not. The results have gone beyond our highest expectations, and have convinced us that the people are ready and waiting for the extension of this work.

The prospect during the earlier part of 1914 was for a rapid development of the Demonstration-Lecture feature of Women's Institute work during the fall and winter of 1914-15; but after the outbreak of war, the Institutes became so engaged with Red Cross, Belgian Relief and various forms of local relief work that they would not take the time, except at a few centres, for systematic instruction. The Department did not wish to discontinue this excellent feature of work; so urged a few centres to take advantage of the instruction, which has heretofore been given at a small charge, but was this winter offered free of tuition.

Courses in sewing have been given at some twelve points, while instruction in food values and cooking has been given at seven centres. One of the most successful of these was that held at Aylmer, Elgin County, January 26 to February 19, 1915. This course included twenty-six lessons in Domestic Science: sixteen morning lessons planned especially for girls and ten afternoon lessons for the same girls as well as experienced housekeepers. The last six afternoons were devoted to lectures from special instructors in dairying, poultry-raising and gardening. The subjects were arranged after the plan of the Macdonald Institute short course in Domestic Science, the programme for the afternoon lessons including:

1.—Fruit—Typical methods of cooking; combinations; different ways of serving fresh fruit.
2.—Vegetables—Fresh, starchy and dried.
3.—Milk.—Soups, puddings and combinations, with especial relation to infant, children and invalid diet.
4.—Cereals and Cheese.—Various methods of cooking; their high food value compared with other more expensive foods.
5.—Eggs—Correct methods of cooking, variations in methods; storage.
6.—Meat—Roasting and broiling; braised dishes, stews and soups, uses of the different cuts, and food value compared with other foods.
7.—Baking-powder breads.—Yeast. Bread and Fancy Breads.
8.—Cake and little Cakes.
9.—Puddings and Desserts.
10.—Salads.

The morning lessons were arranged in correlation with these, going a little more fully into elementary principles and including such additional subjects as Invalid Cookery, Meat Substitutes, Made-Over Dishes, Hot Supper Dishes, Pastry Croquettes, Table Setting and Serving, etc.

The Aylmer women have reflected credit on their Institute by the business-like way in which they carried out their part of the contract. The Local Institute is required to provide and equip the room where the classes are to be held, and to furnish the supplies required for the demonstrations. They are also required to advertise the course throughout the immediate district. In this case, they rented a club-room in an office block, put in a three-burner oil-stove, a work-table and chairs, and then circulated printed programmes advertising the course. The attendance at the first morning class was 34, with 78 in the afternoon. In a few days this had increased to 86 in the morning, and in the afternoon 200, and some more who couldn't get in. On the last evening a hot supper was given at which the Institute realized enough to pay all the expenses of the course with a considerable surplus for patriotic work. It might also be added that during the course ninety-six new members joined the Institute.

A new feature in short course work was introduced in the form of a written examination for those who had taken the complete series of lessons. This also was an experiment, and the question of writing purely voluntary on the part of the students. The paper set will give some idea of the work covered. The questions were:

1. Explain the uses of proteids, carbohydrates, fats, mineral matter and water in the human system, and name some of our common food stuffs in which each of these principles is found largely.
2. Give the recipe, and explain definitely your method of making any two of the following:
    (a) Tea biscuits.
    (b) Plain pastry and puff pastry.
    (c) Cheese croquettes.
3. Make out suitable menus for the three meals a day for one week in July. (1) For a farm family where there is access to a good kitchen garden, a dairy, eggs, and a beef ring or other fresh meat supply, or (2) for a family of five in town where $400 a year can be spent for the food supply.
4. Explain with *reasons* for your method in each case.
    (a) How you would pan broil a steak.
    (b) How you would make a beef stew.
5. Of what special nutritive or medicinal value is each of the following?
    (1) A salad of green vegetables.
    (2) The same salad with nuts added.
    (3) Beef tea.
    (4) Coarse vegetables like spinach or cabbage, and Graham bread.
    (5) A macaroni and cheese dish.
6. (a) Give definite directions for making
    (1) Any two light desserts.
    (2) Any two hot supper dishes.
    (b) Give five salad combinations.
7. What are the characteristics of a good waitress. Give five general rules to remember in table "serving."

The results of this examination were gratifying indeed. The only means of preparation the girls had was through the lessons, with the use of demonstrations and charts, and the reviewing of the notes they took each day, but the following answers taken from four different papers show something of the thoroughness with which they grasped the ideas.

"Proteid in food is that which builds and repairs worn out tissue. It is found largely in lean meats, eggs, cereals, milk, dried beans, cheese, etc.

"Carbohydrate is that in foods which supplies heat and energy. It is composed of starch and sugar. It is found largely in potatoes, parsnips, beets, grains, etc.

"Fat is that in food which supplies heat and energy to the body. It is found in fat meat, bacon, cream, cheese, etc.

"Mineral matter or mineral salts is of use in the system to build body tissue, blood and muscle and nerves. The lime in food also builds up the bone. The mineral salts also act as regulators. They are found in lettuce, cress, spinach, celery, apples and other fruits. Lime is found in cereals and milk.

"Water.—Its use is to act as a regulator, to flush out the system, and to carry off impurities. It is found largely in vegetables such as onions, lettuce, cabbage, etc., also in raw fruits such as oranges, lemons, apples, peaches, etc.

"Recipe for Puff Paste.
  2c. flour; ¼c. lard; ¾c. butter;
½ teaspoon salt.
  About ¼ c. ice water and 1 teaspoon lemon juice.

"Sift the flour and salt several times to get air into it, and make it light. Add the lard, cutting it in with a knife as well as you can, then finish rubbing it in with the tips of the fingers. Then add the water very gradually, using a knife to mix it through, until the dough is of the right consistency to handle. Put on the bake board, and roll very lightly. When rolled ⅓ inch thick, dot part of the butter over half of it. The butter should be creamed with a spoon until it is waxy, and will work into the dough easily. Fold the paste over, fold again in three layers the other way, and roll again till the butter shines through a little, but not till it begins to come through. Fold it over and put it away to chill. When chilled, roll again, dot butter over half the dough, fold, and roll as before. Do this four or five times, or until you have the butter all worked in. When you roll the paste keep it as nearly square as possible so that it is easy to fold. Roll very lightly. Always roll the one way. Never turn the dough over. Keep it cold. Never use puff paste for the bottom crust of a pie.

"To Pan-broil a Steak.—Have your pan very hot so that when you place your steak in it, it will be quickly seared over, then turn and sear the other side. Be sure to never pick it with a fork so that any of the juices will be lost. After it is seared over, · cook it rather slowly. When it is done sprinkle with salt and a little pepper, and you may rub it over with a little butter and lemon juice.

"Reasons.—Sear it quickly so that the little tubes will be sealed over, and all the juices will be retained in the meat. Do not sprinkle salt on at first, for it will draw out the juices. Do not turn with a fork else you allow some of the juices to escape. Finish cooking slowly so as not to toughen the proteids."

One of the answers to the question about the special medicinal or nutritive value of certain foods was:—

"A salad of Green Vegetables.— The green vegetables such as lettuce or other above ground vegetables have a great amount of mineral salts in them. Therefore when eating green vegetables this would purify the blood, and would also help to clear out the system.

"The same salad with nuts in it.— Nuts and especially walnuts are great in food value having so much proteid and fat. So therefore if we had nuts in a green vegetable salad, we would get the fat and proteid besides the mineral matter, and it would be a nourishing dish as well as a medicinal dish.

"Beef tea.—When making beef tea our main idea is to get all the food we can out of the meat into the water, therefore beef tea would be very nourishing if we left the flakes of proteid in it. It is also very good for a sick patient, as there isn't hardly any digesting to do. If the proteid is strained out, the beef tea is only a stimulant and has no nourishment in it.

"Coarse vegetables such as spinach or cabbage, and Graham bread.— These are all valuable for the cellulose that is in them, that is the fibrous material. For example if you scrape a turnip and then squeeze the pulp through a cloth, the cellulose would be the particles left in the cloth. It is indigestible, but forms a bulk in the intestine which stimulates the muscles and helps carry away the waste and therefore helps to overcome constipation. We should take a lot of these foods mentioned.

"Macaroni and Cheese.—Cheese is about one-third proteid and one-third fat. Macaroni is made up of nearly all starch. Therefore this would be a well-balanced dish and very nourishing."

But while we may be most enthusiastic over the possibilities of this work among the young women living out of reach of any other form of technical education, not so much for the specific information given, as that it starts an intelligent interest in things of the home and inspires a desire to make a profession of housekeeping—we appreciate just as much the immediate value to the women who have charge of homes now. The interest which the clever, capable, experienced women of the community have taken in this course, promises that it may become one of the most practical and far reaching lines of college extension work yet undertaken in Canada.

———

Many people do not plant trees because it requires so many years for them to grow to maturity; there are more who are selfish and not willing to go to the trouble of planting trees because they feel that they will not get much benefit out of them. The right view for us to take is that we should do those things which not only help ourselves, but which also add to the comfort and happiness of those who come after us. Boys and girls who plant trees will live to enjoy them and at the same time they will have the satisfaction of knowing that they are doing something which will benefit others for many years to come.—*Charles W. Fairbanks.*

———

I love sunshine, the blue sky, trees, flowers, mountains, green meadows, sunny brooks, the ocean when its waves softly ripple along the sandy beach, or when pounding the rocky cliffs with its thunder and roar, the birds of the field, waterfalls, the rainbow, the dawn, the noonday, and the evening sunset—but children above them all. Trees, plants, flowers, they are always educators in the right direction, they always make us happier and better, and if well grown they speak of loving care and respond to it as far as it is in their power; but in all this world there is nothing so appreciative as children, these sensitive, quivering creatures of sunshine, smiles, showers and tears.—*Luther Burbank.*

———

Hon. Duncan Marshall, Minister of Agriculture for Alberta, at a horse show luncheon recently held at Edmonton, Alta., in speaking of a visit he paid to Belgium before the devastation, said the rule in Belgium was that where animals winning prizes were sold out of the country, the prizes were to be returned. Mr. Marshall thought the rule might profitably be applied in Alberta, as it would have a tendency to keep the best stock at home.

PART III

Provincial Departments of Education

INFORMATION SUPPLIED BY OR THROUGH OFFICIALS OF PROVINCIAL
DEPARTMENTS OF EDUCATION

DOMESTIC SCIENCE IN THE SCHOOLS.

NOVA SCOTIA

BY A. H. MACKAY, B.A., SUPERINTENDENT OF EDUCATION

DOMESTIC Science was first introduced into the schools of Nova Scotia in 1897. In 1900 the Training Department, in affiliation with the Provincial Normal College at Truro, was established for the training of teachers. Ever since that time all the teachers graduating from the Provincial Normal College have taken an elementary course in either Domestic Science or Mechanic Science. The Domestic Science Teachers' Training Course was also established at the same time by the Board of School Commissioners for the town of Truro, in affiliation with the Provincial Normal College, and with the approval of the Council of Public Instruction, for the purpose of furnishing a thorough training to those who wish to become teachers of Domestic Science. The following courses of study are conducted at the Truro School of Domestic Science: Food and cookery; household chemistry and bacteriology; first aids and home nursing; hygiene and home sanitation; laundry textiles and needlework; household economics, including marketing and accounts. This school is open, free of cost, to all who hold a first-class license, or a teacher's pass, or the

Provincial High School Course of Grade Eleven, and on the Science of Grades 9, 10 and 11· Others will be admitted by special arrangement.

Since the year 1900, grants, not to exceed $300 per school, may be earned from the Provincial Funds, the grant being fifteen cents, for each two hour session, per pupil. This is authorized by section 74 of the Education Act.

During the school year ended July, 1914, the expenditure on Domestic Science was $11,254.33, of which $4,747.65 was from the Provincial treasury.

As the number of teachers attending the Normal College has every year been increasing—318 last year— we have been considering the policy of separating from the joint school and erecting an additional building on the Normal College grounds; plans and estimates were prepared for the consideration of the Government, but the difficulty of finding enough money prevented the plans from being carried out.

In the meantime, the College of Agriculture (about a mile distant) devoted a portion of the funds received from THE AGRICULTURAL IN-

362

struction Act grant to erect a special building for courses' in Domestic Science under its own special direction as a part of the general work of the Agricultural College. It is now being proposed to share the use of this building with the Provincial Normal College for any further extension required. The only drawback is the greater inconvenience of arranging a working time table with class rooms a mile away, as compared with those at present which are on the Normal College grounds.

To sum up: our policy of requiring all the female teachers graduating from the Provincial Normal College to take an elementary practical course in Domestic Science, and our policy of Domestic Science Training School preparing teachers for the special Domestic Science diploma (all of which have been in full operation since 1900) will still be continued with extension of accommodation and enlargement of training.

In addition the College of Agriculture is making preparation for the addition of Domestic Science courses to its various other courses under the special direction of Principal Cumming and its own faculty of Instruction. It will necessarily be further enlarged for this purpose.

NEW BRUNSWICK

BY FLETCHER PEACOCK, DIRECTOR OF MANUAL TRAINING AND DOMESTIC SCIENCE

NO money from the Federal grant has been spent on the teaching of Domestic Science in the public schools of New Brunswick. At the summer course for teachers held at Woodstock, N.B., in 1914, a very limited course was provided in this subject, and the teacher was paid from funds provided under The Agricultural Instruction Act.

Practically all the cities and towns in New Brunswick maintain Domestic Science departments in connection with their public schools. The Government pays the teacher in each case an annual grant of two hundred dollars and bears half the cost for the equipment of the class room. None of the villages or country sections have taken up the subject yet, although our Education Act provides for Government assistance should they wish to do so.

In about half of our Domestic Science Schools the subject is taught to grades six to eleven inclusive. In the remaining ones only grades six to eight inclusive are provided for. In all cases each student takes one two-hour lesson per week in plain sewing, cookery, or laundry work.

The Department of Education of New Brunswick recognizes and employs the teachers certificated in Domestic Science by the following schools: Macdonald Institute, Guelph, Ont.; Massey-Trebble School of Household Science, Toronto; Macdonald College, Que.; Mt. Allison College, Sackville, N.B., and Acadia College, Wolfville, N.S. In most cases our teachers have had Normal training and experience in grade teaching before they specialized in Household Science. After teaching the latter subject for a year or more many avail themselves of the summer courses offered at Columbia University, New York.

The method of teaching followed is wholly practical. Each pupil has her own individual equipment and works out her problem independently under the teacher's supervision. Class instruction is given by the teacher in her demonstrations at the beginning of each lesson. It is the aim of the teachers to make the work of the greatest possible utility and to make it relate as directly as may be to the actual work of the homes of the pupils.

· QUEBEC

BY REV. O. E. MARTIN

THERE are now 45 schools of Domestic Science in the province of Quebec. ·Most of them have, so to speak, been established by the provincial Department of Agriculture and all· of them receive special encouragement from the department. The object of these schools is to make good house-keepers of our girls, to make them proficient in women's handicraft, to teach them habits of order, economy, simplicity and discrimination. To help them to carry out this programme, the Department of Agriculture grants to each school a yearly subvention of $300 which is to be· spent · on · organization ·and management.

All these schools, with the exception of two, the one annexed to the Macdonald College of St. Anne de Bellevue and the other in Montreal are managed by nuns of various orders.

These worthy sisters, in order to become more proficient in their work, have not hesitated to take special courses and to secure the required diploma. At some of the schools, the Principals have even secured the services of lay teachers, of well known ability, in order to give more. complete and more efficient training.

Each year since these schools were established the teachers of domestic science have been invited by the provincial Department of Agriculture to meet at the domestic science normal schools of Roberval and St. Pascal, to take special courses in domestic economy and agriculture, in order to prepare themselves better to perform their task.

All teachers from all quarters have responded to these invitations and nuns of all ages have been seen on the benches of these normal schools, like ordinary pupils, following the lessons with close attention in order to impart the same information to the pupils of their own schools.

The programme of the domestic science. schools includes instruction and practical demonstration in the following subjects:—

Cooking; general house-keeping; economical self-keeping; cutting; sewing; darning; mending; folding clothes, linen, etc.; pressing suits keeping of the wardrobe; laundry work; ironing; starching; spinning; weaving; netting; house-keeping; milking; care of milk; skimming; manufacture of butter and small cheese; gardening; bee-keeping, fruit culture; poultry keeping; making preserves; home medicine; inspection of various tissues, etc.

EQUIPMENT

The following equipment is found in the schools: A special kitchen and kitchen utensils, charts showing the various meat animals on foot or cut up; very good tables showing the composition of the various animal or vegetable matter used for human consumption, book of receipes, etc. The equipment of the sewing room is as follows: Linen closets, tables, sewing machines, blackboards, squares, measures, etc. The laundry and ironing room are also generally well equipped.

In addition to the washing machines, run by motor, there are other implements of more common use, such as wooden or galvanized iron tubs, washing boards, etc., for the use of the pupils.

Most of the schools also endeavour as far as their financial means permit, to keep before the pupils by means of good sets of charts, the articles which they will have to handle in practice. General botany, horticulture, arboriculture, agriculture,

bee-keeping, have of course a prominent place in these charts.

The general house-keeping work
gives ample daily practice in cleanliness, order and good taste. But the
thousand and one details of house-
work do not prevent the sisters from
teaching their pupils the knowledge
in outside work that a skilful house-
keeper should possess. The activity
of the pupils find ample scope for
action in the stable at milking time,
the garden, the poultry house, the
apiary and the orchard.

Each school also has a modern
poultry house, and some have splendid flocks of fowls. The preparation
of grain and mashes, the cleaning of
nests and roosts, the ventilation,
etc., etc., are all part of the daily
programme. With the poultry house
there are also the incubator, the
brooder and the care of eggs and
chicks. The pupils, at least the
most advanced, know all about these
things. But they are quite as much
interested in gardening work as in
poultry work. Most of them take a
real delight in conducting a hot-bed,

examining the seeds, seeding, preparing the soil, transplanting, weed-
ing, etc. The apiary, the small
orchard and the growing of flowers
are also the object of the attentive
care of the pupils.

In all domestic science schools the
teachers lay great stress on the importance of cleanliness in the production and conservation of milk.
The pupils are also trained in economy; they acquire habits of order,
cleanliness and sound judgment .

Domestic book-keeping is also
continually practised.

The total attendance at the domestic science schools of the province,
including the schools at the Macdonald College and the one at Montreal, was 4,322 pupils. These
schools were inspected last summer
by a priest of the archdiocese of
Quebec, under the direction of
Honourable Mr. Caron, Minister of
Agriculture.

The selection of a member of the
clergy for this work has been viewed
with favour by many people.

ONTARIO

COMPLIED FROM DEPARTMENTAL PUBLICATIONS.

IN a general way the Department
of Education for Ontario at-
taches great importance to the
subject of Household Science and
provides facilities for its practice.
It is the intention of the Minister,
Hon. R. A. Pyne, to encourage the
study throughout the province both
in urban and rural schools. Instruction is given at day and evening
classes where opportunity offers.
A regulation provided is that no
grant shall be made for household
science unless at least provision has
been made for sewing, cookery, sanitation and hygiene. When the time
of one teacher is occupied for five
and a half hours of each of five days
in the week the grant is $120 per
annum. When it is less the amount

is decreased and when more it is
increased. In the distribution of the
grant it is required that the maximum
recognized value of the equipment
for the different departments shall
be as follows:—

Cookery, Sanitation and Hygiene..	$500
Hand and Machine Sewing........	250
Laundry Work....................	150
Library..........................	100

The Department also pays the
following proportions of the total
salaries of the Household Science
night classes: In cities with a population of 150,000 and over, one-
sixth; in other cities, one-third; in
towns, one-half, and in villages,
two-thirds.

For the qualification of teachers,

spring and summer courses are held at the Household Science Department, University of Toronto, leading to certificates in Elementary Household Science. The work for a certificate is covered in one spring session or in two consecutive summer sessions. Students who are entitled to qualify for certificates are:—

Grade A Normal School students who have passed the final examination of the Normal Schools and have taken the prescribed course in manual training at the Ontario Agricultural College, Guelph, or in household science at the University of Toronto, and have passed the prescribed final examination.

Other Normal School students who have taken the High School course in manual training or in household science and have passed the final examination.

Teachers who possess first, second or third class certificates, who have taken the prescribed courses in household science at Toronto University or the Ontario Agricultural College at Guelph, and have passed the prescribed final examinations.

Interim ordinary certificates in household science are granted to those who have taken the household science course at the Macdonald Institute at Guelph.

Special provision is made for village or rural schools unable to make use of the general regulations by which grants are conferred; a first grant of $50 being made for qualified instruction and a second grant of $30 on approval by the Minister. A grant of $30 will also be added to the salary of the teacher

on a report of satisfaction by the inspector of household science.

The course includes:—

The House:—Purpose, location, general ideas concerning use and furnishing rooms, methods of cleaning, laundrying, etc.

Foods:—Elements required by the body, sources; food value and digestion of these; analysis of common foods—milk, eggs, meat, fruit, vegetables, cereals; effect of these in food value, digestibility and flavour.

Cookery:—Construction and care of stoves; fuels; principles and practice of each method of cooking—boiling, broiling, steaming, frying, baking; food combustions; flour mixtures; lightening agents; table service.

Bacteriology:—Occurrence and nature of bacteria; sanitation based on this knowledge; preservation of foods.

Home Nursing:—The ideal sick room (location, furnishing, ventilation, heating), care of the patient (bath, bed, clothing, food).

Sewing:—Study and application of different stitches, basting, running, stitching, back stitching, combination stitch, overcasting, top sewing, blanket, herringbone, feather-stitching, mending, darning, button-holing, hemming, doll's apron.

In the advanced course marketing entertaining and the keeping of household accounts are added to a review and progress of the first year's work.

Lectures and demonstrative lessons are given from time to time at different points.

MANITOBA

BY R. FLETCHER, B.A., DEPUTY MINISTER OF EDUCATION

THE Department of Education in this province makes a grant of 50 per cent of the amount spent in equipping a department for Household Science work, with the proviso that our maximum grant shall not exceed $400 for one department. We also pay the same grant per day in the case of special teachers of Household Science as we pay in the case of the ordinary teacher in the grades. We have been endeavouring to secure a larger daily grant for these special teachers, but so far we have not succeeded. We are urging our schools to introduce Household Science wherever possible, and we have made fair headway in the matter of sewing, which is not an expensive course to introduce, and which the majority of our regular day school teachers are equipped to teach.

We have advocated the grouping of two or more towns or villages, and the employment of a special teacher for the group; and I think we should accomplish something along these lines if we had funds to enable us to make a reasonable grant towards the salary of such a teacher.

SASKATCHEWAN

BY D. P. McCOLL, B.A., DEPUTY MINISTER OF EDUCATION

RESPECTING the policy of the Department of Education in the matter of instruction in Household Science I may say that it has been incorporated into our courses of study for both public and high schools. In the lower grades of the public schools the main stress is laid on sewing; in the senior grades and in high schools on cookery.

In order to encourage boards of trustees to make provision for this subject, grants are paid by the department to schools that provide the necessary equipment and accommodation and give satisfactory instruction therein.

In so far as the teachers-in-training at Normal Schools are concerned Household Science is regarded as an essential part of the course of training. In addition to the training they receive at the Normal School, courses are being prepared for their guidance upon taking charge of schools and particularly schools in rural districts where special efforts are being made to direct teachers in this work under such conditions as exist in rural communities. It is the intention of the department to keep in touch with the work through inspection, circulation of bulletins, circulating libraries, etc.

In order to more thoroughly organize the work in all the classes of schools and give the subject the attention its importance deserves a directress for the province has recently been appointed and she will enter upon her duties at an early date. In addition to instruction at the Normal school these duties will include the general supervision, inspection and direction of the work in schools, attendance at teachers' institutes and conventions, and the taking of such steps as may be necessary to make Household Science a vital part of our educational system.

ALBERTA

BY JAMES C. MILLER, B.SC., PH.D., DIRECTOR OF TECHNICAL EDUCATION

THE introduction of household arts including domestic science and domestic art into the course of study for the public schools of Alberta was officially provided for at the time of the revision of the course of studies for public schools in 1911. In both Calgary and Edmonton a beginning had already been made and several centres were in operation. While at this time the work was given a place on the course of study and the board were granted the permission to spend the necessary money to have the work carried on, no provision was made for special government grants. At the beginning of 1913 departments of household arts were organized in each of the provincial normal schools. Miss McCaig, formerly instructor in household arts in the North Bay Normal School, Ontario, took charge of the department in the Calgary Normal School and Miss Margaret Stewart, formerly instructor in household arts in the Calgary public schools, took charge of the department in the Camrose Normal School. During the normal school course the students are given two hours' instruction per week in domestic science and one hour instruction per week in domestic art. The shortness of the normal school course makes it impossible to do more than to introduce the students to the subject and give them an idea of its place and value in the education of children. When the supply of teachers available is such as to make it possible to lengthen the regular normal school course—there are indications that this will be the case in the course of a year—a much more satisfactory course in these subjects for teachers in training can be provided.

In order to give the teachers additional training in the special subjects including domestic science and domestic art the Summer School for Teachers was organized in 1913 at the Provincial University. The courses are planned in such a way as to make two successive summers' work in a given subject a complete unit. The total attendance at the Summer School for 1913 was 80, and for 1914, 150. Sixty-nine teachers have completed one summer's work in domestic science or domestic art. A summer school enrolment of over 300 is expected for 1915 and it is probable that a large number will take the first year's work in household arts and that practically all of those who have completed the first summer's work will undertake the second summer's work in the subject.

The development of the work in full has up to the present been limited to the cities. In both Calgary and Edmonton the number of centres and instructors has been increased so as to make it possible for all of the girls of Grades VII and VIII to receive their instruction in this subject each week. Both Medicine Hat and Lethbridge provided one domestic science centre and employed the services of a specialist.

In the autumn of 1914 the policy of the Provincial Government in regard to technical education as a whole was more definitely formulated and a general scheme of provincial aid for the development of instruction along technical lines was outlined. As an integral part of the scheme provision was made for a special grant for the encouragement of instruction in household arts. The schedule of grants in so far as it affects this subject is as follows:

(A) In rural and village school districts:

1. To the school board: An annual grant equal to 50 per cent of the value of approved equipment up to a maximum grant of $15.

(2) To the teacher: An annual grant of $20.

(B) In any school district including a town or city in which fewer than 30 teachers are employed:

(1) To the school board: An annual grant equal to 10 per cent of the value of the approved equipment up to a maximum grant of $100 exclusive of grants earned under Section 18 of The School Grants' Act.

(2) To the teacher responsible for such instruction and giving full time service to the board: An annual grant of $50.

(C) In any school district including a town or city in which at least 30 teachers are employed:

(1) To the school board, for each instructor or supervisor of Household Science and Art in the employ of the board and giving full time service in these subjects: An annual grant equal to that earned for the board by a teacher in charge of a regular classroom. (Section 18—The School Grants Act).

NOTE: "Section 18 of the School Grants Act provides that all the teachers of special subjects shall rank as regular teachers for the purposes of the government grants." This means that a teacher giving her full time to household arts will earn for the school board as much grant as a teacher in charge of one of the regular classrooms.

Plans for the introduction of this subject into the high school course of study are now under consideration and definite steps in this direction will be taken during the present year.

The development of instruction in household arts in the rural, village, town and city public schools and in the high schools, special provincial assistance to encourage the introduction of the subject and to help in maintenance, the extension of the courses in household arts now offered at the normal schools, to the further development of the work of the Summer School for Teachers, and as soon as possible the provision for the training of specialists, are the main features of the plan of the Department of Education for the further development of this division of educational service.

BRITISH COLUMBIA
BY ALEXANDER ROBINSON, SUPERINTENDENT OF EDUCATION

IN thirteen cities of this province Domestic Science is taught in thirty-two centres.

As we have had no means of training Domestic Science teachers, all our instructors come from the Eastern States, the Eastern Provinces, or from the United Kingdom. The Normal School, however, just erected in Victoria, has the necessary equipment and housekeeping rooms for such training, and this may be undertaken at some future date.

DOMESTIC SCIENCE REGULATIONS

The regulations for Domestic Science are as follows:—

Every instructor must hold a British Columbia instructors' certificate of qualification.

Each applicant for this certificate must have had two years' training, hold a satisfactory diploma from one of the recognized training colleges in Canada, the United States, or the United Kingdom, and hold a public school teachers' certificate, or have had other approved professional standing. Every application for a certificate must be accompanied with the usual fee of $5 and a satisfactory testimonial certifying to the good moral character of the applicant.

Rules relating to Domestic Science centres:—

1. Where Domestic Science centres are established, attendance is compulsory and must be continuous throughout the school-year. The hours of instruction in Domestic Science shall be as defined in Article 1 of the Rules and Regulations for the government of Public Schools.

Girls, from distant schools, in attendance at the morning session, may be dismissed at 11.45.

2. A three years' course of Domestic Science should be taken in the public schools.

3. All pupils in the entrance class and in the two classes below the entrance class shall take Domestic Science. Classes doing parallel work in other subjects shall do parallel work in Domestic Science.

4. Attendance registers, records of lessons, an inventory of equipment, and a visitors' book must be kept and be open for inspection at all times.

5. Expense sheets for food and other materials, exclusive of heating, lighting, and permanent equipment, should be sent to the secretary of the Board at the end of each month, also an attendance sheet.

6. Only one course of work will be recognized for all the schools in the one city.

7. Domestic Science instructors shall be subject to the same general regulations as Public School Teachers.

8. The principal of the public school at which a Domestic Science centre is situated shall have supervision over the general discipline of all classes in attendance at that centre.

9. Plans for Domestic Science buildings must be submitted to the Department of Education for approval.

10. All courses of work in Domestic Science must be submitted to the Education Department for approval. Needlework to intermediate grade and senior grade pupils may be included in the course.

FIRST-YEAR COURSE

Home management; home nursing, theory and practice; laundrywork, theory and practice.

SECOND-YEAR COURSE

Junior cookery, theory and practice.

THIRD-YEAR COURSE

Senior cookery, theory and practice.

Diplomas are awarded by the Department of Education to pupils who complete the course prescribed for Domestic Science. Female candidates for high school entrance examinations from schools in which instruction has been given in Domestic Science must hold Domestic Science diplomas or fulfil departmental requirements as to attendance and work.

To the Board of School Trustees in rural districts, and to the Municipal Corporation of any municipality whose board of School Trustees provide suitable accommodation for Domestic Science in connection with the school or schools under their jurisdiction, the Council of Public Instruction grants a sum of not less than three-fourths of the total amount expended for the necessary equipment.

The total per capita grant for school teachers is also paid for Domestic Science teachers, viz.:—

To cities of the 1st class	$360
To cities of the 2nd class	425
To cities of the 3rd class	465
Rural districts	480

In addition to this, a supplementary grant of one-dollar for every dollar by which the salary of the teacher is increased is also paid; but in no case must this supplementary grant to be paid by the Government exceed one hundred dollars.

SUMMER SCHOOL FOR TEACHERS

At the Summer School for teachers held from 6th July to 1st August, 1914, we had 113 students attending with four instructors in charge. Good practical courses in needlework and cooking were covered. Lectures were given on foods, sanitation, personal hygiene, the home and household decoration, textiles, etc.

Return transportation was paid from the homes of the students, and one dollar per day towards living expenses.

Thus it will be seen that the Department of Education considers it important that instruction in Domestic Science be given to every girl who attends the ordinary day school. They also look with favour on the instructor with an education liberal enough to use the history lesson of the school to throw a light on the suffering of the races through ignorance of hygiene; the geography lesson, to draw attention to the influence of environment of food, clothing, occupation, and disease; the physics to show the understanding of the problems of ventilation, heating, cooking, and cleaning; and the subject of Domestic Science as embracing everything which makes for right living and the beautifying of human lives.

RELATIONSHIP OF THE SCHOOL GARDEN TO THE CLASS ROOM

NOVA SCOTIA

BY L. A. DeWOLFE, M. SC., DIRECTOR RURAL SCIENCE SCHOOLS

THE school garden helps the class-room in, at least, two ways. First: it gives that healthful exercise so necessary to school children, at a time when they most need it. In this, too, it furnishes variety, and breaks the monotony of school life.

But the second and most important consideration, is that it vitalizes school work. The principles of mechanical drawing are mastered while drawing a plan of the garden to scale. Business methods are learned when buying the seeds; and, later in the year, when banking the profits. Many a boy gets his first lesson in good manners and community welfare when he is taught not to walk in his pupil-neighbour's garden plot.

The lessons on soil physics, in connection with conservation of moisture, make a tangible introduction to general physics in the class-room. Identification of weed-seedlings and garden seedlings is the first step towards field botany. The control of these leads at once to economic botany.

What better arithmetic problems can be given than the boy's own problems to find how much seed or how much fertilizer his garden requires, when tabulated amounts are per acre?

The insect pests furnish good lessons on Entomology. The insecticides and fungicides form a natural basis for lessons in chemistry. The covering of plants to protect from late spring frosts introduces a phase of physical geography not often well taught.

The written descriptions of garden operations furnish unlimited exercise in English composition. No drawing lessons could be more attractive than those based on the garden and its products; and no reading should be more suitable than some of the best garden compositions written by the students.

Commercial geography will, perhaps, be helped more than any one subject.

In the hands of the skilful teacher, the school garden is the connecting link between the school and the real world.

NEW BRUNSWICK

BY R. P. STEEVES, M.A., DIRECTOR ELEMENTARY AGRICULTURAL EDUCATION

THE school garden is an outdoor work-shop or laboratory to be made use of by the teacher in the process of general education of the pupils. In its construction and care are affiliated physical activity, mental development and aesthetic training. Through the senses the mind is constantly receiving impressions which must stimulate observation, thought, and judgment and which wisely guided lead to intelligent expression and application. The succession of seasons, the adaptation of supply to need, the influence of climate, the relation between labour and providence, the dependence of animal life upon plants, and of these latter upon soil conditions, among the most important of which is the presence of numberless, infinitesimal bacteria, all furnish problems most intricate and difficult, but adequate for mental culture. Moreover the concrete consideration of such topics affords opportunity for moral and spiritual development since the wisdom of the beneficent Creator is traced in every manifestation of nature illustrated in the garden and its environment. Talks by the teacher in the school room about nature may exert an influence for good upon the young, but actual participation with nature in the open air, where her laws are being exemplified, and her varying moods and phenomena are being observed, elevates all to be co-workers as it were with the Divine. Individual effort is directed, character is exalted and education is enriched by a fund of information obtained at first hand. Incidentally through such outdoor work also the schoolroom instruction is enlivened and enforced by illustrations pertinent because they appeal to conditions and actions with which the pupils are familiar.

The school garden may be made to occupy an important place in the teaching of the usual schoolroom subjects. The purpose and object of education is the production of good citizenship. It is by what we are, and how we do what we engage in, that we prove our position in the nation. Example and practice establish precept and theory.

The first element of success to secure in any school is interest. This must be obtained through the natural unfolding of the child's powers. Children are interested in life, living things, which appeal to them through their senses. Through an interest thus secured we may awaken in the child a realization of need to know how to solve arithmetical questions, to use language with clearness and accuracy, to properly spell words used, to be able to make correct drawings and to learn the geographical and historical features of his native place. The school garden furnishes the living objects which appeal to the child's interest. Through his contact with it many varieties of arithmetical problems arise, from those of the simplest fundamental nature to intricate questions of commercial transactions. How can one better learn the principles and application of measurements than by actually making the measurements of land in the open? What better way to acquire the principles of bookkeeping than by actually keeping a set of books that represent the work of a season in a school garden, or home plot?

No better incentive to learn to draw can be afforded than for the child to realize his need of preserving the impression made upon his mind by some object of nature. The object to be drawn must be something to him, or he will not recognize the value of committing to paper his idea of it. If that drawing inadequately represents his idea, at once he appreciates his need to give more careful attention to his teacher's instruction. Later, his ability to picture the varieties of form represented in the school garden will attest to the quality of the instruction he has received.

The study of language must ever take up much time in the school. Ordinary methods of teaching are likely to lack interest because of being largely abstract. It is not the word or the arrangement of words that will attract the pupil's attention unless he realizes that his own effort falls short of conveying to others the thought in his mind. Oral should precede written expression. Impressions should be made on the mind before expression is attempted. Personal knowledge comes largely through observation and physical effort. We talk best, most naturally, about what we know, what we are interested in. Nature study exercises, through the school garden, supply the best avenues for personal knowledge through the child's observation. By using the child's language descriptive of what he is interested in, of what he knows, the teacher is able to demonstrate successfully the fundamental rules of composition and their application in his every day life. Illustrations taken from books may later serve to confirm decisions reached. It is, however, through the child's own language made use of as a basis for composition lessons that the best results can be achieved. Language is a medium for conveying our thought to others. When it is studied with that practical view in sight, the value of such study takes on a new significance.

The monotony of indoor school exercises which have to do with mental training alone, may be relieved through the school garden lessons and activities participated in by both pupils and teacher. It is by the mingling of the active and the mental, by the outdoor and the indoor, that the best results are obtained at the least expenditure of time and nerve.

The school garden furnishes a link between the school and the home in that it makes use of the home occupations for an educative purpose. The school premises indicate the high water mark of educational appreciation in the district. The school is ground common to all. Whatever succeeds in uniting the people in a common effort to improve will be found most beneficial. If the school grounds are dilapidated and neglected the tone of the community may naturally be expected to be sluggish and downward in tendency. Many school grounds which, before a school garden was established, were unfenced are now neatly enclosed by woven wire. The school garden has contributed its part to making the grounds attractive and has thus demonstrated its value in the education of the community.

On Arbor Day, which usually comes in May, and on Empire Day, opportunities are afforded for all the residents of the community to contribute their part in improving the school property. The teachers with the pupils contribute their part. We cannot be loyal to the Empire unless we are first loyal to our own community. We need to faithfully express our loyalty by acts. The month of May is, in country districts, a very busy time for the people; but a half day spent in connection with their school, living with their children at the school, will yield a more bountiful harvest in developing a community life sentiment than any other crop that could be put in in the same amount of time on their lands at home. Our duty as citizens in the district is to make life happier, more attractive and more social for the children while they are still at school. The best country district is the one where the teacher unites with the pupils and the parents in regular efforts from time to time to make a real centre of attraction and the school grounds a veritable local beauty spot. The school garden and nature study exercises in the open air are the complement of the indoor mental training. In reading, language, spelling, writing, arithmetic, history and geography they may by correlation and interweaving give energy and purpose to school life. Thus interest will develop as the child passes along through the grades and thus, too, he may be encouraged to remain longer at school securing a broader, more cultural education and more practical withal, because it is being obtained in terms of his daily life and environment.

MANITOBA

BY H. W. WATSON, DIRECTOR ELEMENTARY AGRICULTURAL EDUCATION

THE school garden furnishes the concrete material for the following:—

Arithmetic:—Number of plots in a certain area, allowing for walks; number of ounces of seed for each plot at a certain rate per acre; yield per acre based upon the number of pounds per plot.

Elementary Geometry:—Planning the plots in various sizes and shapes on paper and drawing to a scale.

Drawing and Colourwork:—Concrete specimens are readily obtainable at most seasons of the year.

Composition:—Excellent practice may be obtained in writing descriptions and keeping records.

Farm Bookkeeping:— Children may keep records of various expenditures and receipts in connection with their plots and hence learn the principles of keeping crop records, stock records, etc.

Literature:— Interesting supplementary reading may be obtained in bulletins, farm journals, etc.

Geography:—Maps of the gardens are made, of the school ground, the village, township, county and province. Study of the industries and products of our own locality increases the interest in the study of such for other countries.

Manual Training:—The making of window-boxes, hot-beds, flats, pegs, markers, etc., greatly increases the interest in the use of the common tools.

Botany:—Abundant material may be had during the spring and autumn, and also during the winter, by gathering and preserving such as will be required.

General Nature Study:—Concrete specimens may be had for the study of plants, birds, insects, wild animals, etc., and all in their relation to agriculture.

Elementary Physics:—Valuable lessons may be learned in mechanics, heat, light, moisture, each in relation to the practical affairs of life.

BRITISH COLUMBIA

BY J. W. GIBSON, M.A., DIRECTOR, ELEMENTARY AGRICULTURAL EDUCATION

SOME one has called the school garden the out-of-doors laboratory of the school, by which we would understand that it is a place for doing experimental work, making observations and recording results. Gardening is to the boys and girls of public school age largely experimental, and this is one of the reasons why they are so much interested in it; moreover, the knowledge gained in this way, at first hand and as the result of the pupils' work and observation, seems to be so much more real to them than that which they gain from reading and class room interpretation which too often is the teacher's interpretation for the credulous pupils. But we would do well to keep in mind that it is not so much the facts acquired by the child, whether by his own discovery or from reading, that are important but rather the relationship of facts, that is, interpretation. This latter and more important process of interpretation is the result of reflection following on observation. The class room is the best place for the completion of garden lessons. The teacher directs the processes leading to such understanding by recalling the observations made by the different pupils in the class (oral language work for the pupils) and by good questioning stimulating reflection, thus leading the pupils to arrive at their own conclusions or else revealing to them the need of making further observation. These class room conversations or discussions (I hesitate to use the term "lessons" because of certain unhallowed memories which the term recalls), are or can be made as interesting to the class as were their previous observations in the garden. There is a lot of truth in the remark made by some one who

understood children and who also understood teaching, to the effect that "a child delights in the discovery of a new relationship as much as in the discovery of a new object." The class room then is the place where the "adjourned business meeting" is held, where the reports of "committees" of investigation are presented, accepted, amended in committee of the whole or rejected, conclusions arrived at and resolutions finally passed.

Then again the class room discussion of plans and possibilities helps to give the pupils a purpose and point of view which aids them "to get somewhere" in the work which they decide to undertake. It affords the introduction and perchance the invocation as it also pronounces the benediction on the part performed in the garden.

Space will not permit of even the briefest consideration of how other school subjects, such as reading, spelling, composition, nature study, geography, arithmetic, drawing and all the rest, can with great advantage be correlated with school gardening. The garden and experiences in it become the great centre of reality for the child. These various subjects merely result from the different types of reaction and expression of the child mind. Herein these formal subjects find a place and application. They are as the "tools" that the child has to learn to use in fashioning the "raw materials" which he daily and hourly acquires through experience or sense perception, and each would be useless without the other. The garden stands for child experience and the class room has stood too much for "subjects" and formal discipline. Let us bring them together.

TEACHING AGRICULTURE IN THE RURAL SCHOOLS OF QUEBEC

BY JEAN-CHARLES MAGNAN, B.S.A., DISTRICT REPRESENTATIVE

AS stated in the program of the Catholic schools of the province, " In rural schools the most important thing is to keep the thought of the pupils on Agricultural Subjects." The teachers must be made to understand the influence that may be exerted through object lessons, lectures, dictations, problems of arithmetic, etc. The ideas given in these lessons or exercises fix them-

For this purpose the official program of the Catholic schools of our province prescribes teaching of the elements of agriculture from the third to the eighth year, inclusively. This information which should be given as object lessons includes the following : " Practical information on domestic animals; poultry; useful animals for the farmers; fruit trees ; forest trees; the chief fodder plants of the district; the chief

GROUP OF SCHOOL GARDENERS AT ST. CASIMIR, QUE.

selves in the minds of the pupil, they monopolize the greater part of his intelligence during the years of primary school. If agricultural subjects are often mentioned, an indelible impression will be made, and useful lessons may be taught without overloading the program of studies. Thus will be created, without any loss of time, this agricultural atmosphere so desirable in country schools.

industrial plants of the locality; some ornamental plants; farming implements; cereals, the chief cereals of the locality, sowing, care and harvesting; general information on agricultural machinery and on farm buildings." (Third and fourth years, elementary course.)

The general program of class work for the modern course (fifth and sixth years) and for the academic course (seventh and eighth years) is the following: "Practical informa-tion on soils and soil treatment; manures and fertilizers; agricultural work; feeding, breeding and hy-giene of domestic animals; agri-cultural machinery and farm build-ings. Soil and sub-soil; drainage. Fertilizers: manures; commercial fertilizers. Ploughing, deep plough-ing; various implements of tillage. Rotations: Feeding live stock; meat production; breeding and im-provement of live stock; qualities of the various species of farm ani-mals. Dairying industry: milk, butter, cheese. Poultry. Live stock hygiene. The enemies of the farmer; the friends of the farmer; beekeeping. Agricultural book-keeping; rural economy. Sowing of cereals; care of cereal crops; perma-nent meadows; artificial meadows. Vegetable garden ; fruit garden ; apple culture; arboriculture and horticulture. Hoed crops and fod-der crops. Farm buildings; farmer's hygiene. Harvesting of cereals. Advantages of farming as an occupa-tion."

The "Manuel d'Agriculture Il-lustré" of the Brothers of Christian Instruction is used as a text book, in addition to the object lessons. This manual, well illustrated, helps to give to the children a liking for the farm. It is used by a large number of teachers in the rural schools.

The scholars also keep an agri-cultural copy-book containing a summary of the lessons taught in the class. Some of our schools also have an agricultural museum, which is

made use of in teaching. So much for the class work in agriculture. And this class work, when skillfully conducted, leads quite naturally to the practice of agriculture, that is, to the school garden.

In school gardens the pupils do the work themselves. Not only do they help the teacher in caring for the garden, but some plots are re-served for them for which they are made entirely responsible.

Seeds, flowers, plants, and other roots are given to the pupils who sow them or plant them after preparing the soil according to the instructions issued by the Department. The school gardening work is thus a means of teaching pupils while affording at the same time a healthy pastime.

Conducted with intelligence, gar-dening work creates a liking for farm work. It has a happy in-fluence on the mind and the health of the children and justifies agri-cultural class work in the eyes of the parents.

In order to maintain constant relation between school work and practical work, there is nothing so useful as "A diary of my garden," in which the pupil keeps a careful record of all the work he does, his impressions, his observations, the difficulties that he has met with, and the results which he has obtained. This relation, which is necessary for the rational teaching of agriculture in the rural schools, is also kept by writing exercises, dictations, prob-lems, etc., bearing on agriculture.

PREPARATION AND MOUNTING OF WEEDS FOR CLASS AND REFERENCE WORK
BY FAITH FYLES, B.A., ASSISTANT BOTANIST, CENTRAL EXPERIMENTAL FARM

THERE is no more interesting study than that of the life history of weeds, if properly undertaken. There is nothing that will interest the student of nature

more than to watch the development of the weed from the seed.

Seeds should be secured in the autumn, cleaned and put in a cool dry place during the winter. If any uncertainty arises as to the exact species, send a whole plant in to the Dominion Botanist, Central Experimental Farm, Ottawa, for identification.

Presuming then that you have on wooden boxes in the class room for the continuation of work, when the supply of seedlings on the blotting paper has been exhausted. Small seeds should be covered with a very thin layer of soil, which should be

PLATE I.   A.   RAGWEED.   B.   BLACK MEDICK IN POD.
           C.   COW CRESS.   D.   MALLOW.
(Drawn by F. Fyles).

hand a good supply of living seed, you are ready to start work in the early spring, when your pupils having received a certain knowledge of botany and botanical terms during the winter, are keen to put it into practice. Scatter the seeds on a square of wet blotting paper on a saucer and cover with another saucer inverted. At the same time, or a few days later, some seeds of the same species may be sown in shallow moderately moist. Drawings and notes should be made as to the swelling of the seed, the rupture of the seed coat, the first appearance of root, shoot, or hypocotyl; the development of root-hairs, the unfolding of the cotyledons and many other points of interest. Emphasis should be laid on the point that careful drawings of each stage of growth ought to be made by the pupils. Nothing will add more to

PLATE II.   UPPER ROW—CINQUEFOIL.
LOWER ROW—RAGWEED. .
(Photo by F. W. L. Sladen).

their interest or develop more quickly their power of observation than the effort to make the drawings tell the story. Specimens of the seedlings should be pressed when the cotyledons expand, when the bud appears in their axil, when the first true leaves unfold and at each important subsequent change. These later stages of development will be seen in the plants in the boxes, or better still in the school garden, if a small space can be spared for the study of noxious weeds.

FIELD WORK

If it is not permissible to grow weeds in the school garden, the more mature plants must be studied in the field. For field work a light portable press and vasculum are necessary. Fill the press with sheets of felt paper alternating with a double fold of rather heavy weight tissue paper or light weight unglazed wrapping paper. The advantage of the enfolding paper is, that all necessary data

can be written on it, i.e., name, habitat, locality, date and collector's name. These, as well as the plant, will remain undisturbed when the wet felt papers are removed. The felt papers must be changed every day and in the case of succulent plants, as, for instance the sow-thistles, twice a day. This is *absolutely necessary* if you wish to have specimens with a good colour and free from mould. Dry the felt papers in the sun before using them again.

PLATE IV. A SATISFACTORY METHOD OF MOUNTING WEEDS
(Photo by Dr. F. T. Shutt)

Unknown plants should be numbered and a duplicate, similarly numbered put into the vasculum, where it will be kept fresh till its position and name can be determined with the help of a botanical key. The specimens must not be taken out of the press till thoroughly dry.

CHOICE OF SPECIMENS

As success in any line of work depends largely on its general appearance, care should be taken to choose normal, well proportioned,

PLATE III. AN UNSATISFACTORY METHOD OF MOUNTING WEEDS
(Photo by Dr. F. T. Shutt)

average-sized plants, free from disease and insects. Place them in a natural position on the pressing paper and arrange the leaves, buds, flowers and seed-pods in different positions, in order that all important characters may be seen. If the roots are thick, cut them lengthwise and reverse one-half.

MOUNTING THE SPECIMENS

The old way of mounting botanical specimens for demonstration purposes was hardly satisfactory. Gumming the plants to sheets of paper or fastening them with little strips of gummed paper as in the illustration (Plate III) means a tedious loss of time and patience, while the almost immediate result is a soiled, faded, dog-eared and broken object—a blot on the wall. Compare the method in the next illustration (Plate IV). Here is as complete a series of specimens as may be desired, showing the life history of the plant from seed to seed, protected from the atmosphere, unfingered and intact, safe from the destruction of dust and flies, easily and simply prepared. The weeds are put on the cotton batting, and held in place by the glass cover. Some two or three hundred of these cases have been prepared at the Central Farm for use in the Dominion Experimental Farms' exhibits throughout Canada.

(NOTE.—This subject will be continued in the May number of THE AGRICULTURAL GAZETTE in which officials in the several provinces will describe how they prepare and mount specimens of plants for study.—*Editor*.)

Prince Edward County, Ontario, announces school fairs for the fall of 1915 in the townships of Ameliasburg, Hillier, Hallowell, Athol, Sophiasburg, North Marysburgh and South Marysburgh.

The Quebec Journal of Agriculture announces that the agricultural merit competition this year will take place in District No. 1, comprising the counties of Jacques Cartier, Hochelaga, Laval, Two Mountains, Soulanges, Vaudreuil and the parishes and townships of Argenteuil and Terrebonne counties which are not included in the Laurentides. Applications for forms on which entries can be made must be filed with the Minister of Agriculture, Quebec, on or before June 15th.

PART IV

Special Contributions, Reports of Agricultural Organizations, Notes and Publications

THE WORK OF THE CANADIAN SEED GROWERS' ASSOCIATION WITH POTATO CROP

BY L. H. NEWMAN, B.S.A., SECRETARY, OTTAWA, ONT.

THE Canadian Seed Growers' Association was organized in 1904 with a view to encouraging individual farmers in the production and more general use of better seed of the different classes of farm crops. For the first few years the cereal crops received greatest attention, but more recently the potato has come to receive due consideration. The need for systematic work among individual growers, and the opportunity for making substantial gains with this crop is everywhere apparent. We have in Canada a great number of different varieties and strains of potatoes—a condition which results in much confusion and uncertainty. In many districts there are to be found almost as many varieties as there are growers, the result of which is that sooner or later these varieties are almost sure to become more or less mixed. Perhaps a still more serious result of this condition is that buyers find it impossible to purchase any considerable quantity of potatoes of a uniform type at a given point. This is a very serious handicap to a potato growing locality, either where the potatoes are sold for eating or for seed. This condition obtains particularly in Ontario and parts of Quebec. Realizing the need for some special effort in correcting this situation, and knowing that there are many farmers here and there throughout the country who are anxious and willing to do something if given some assistance, the Association devised a system by means of which a grower might systematically select his seed potatoes from year to year with a reasonable assurance of improving the type and being able to offer the trade a pure strain of a distinctive character. The system which has been adopted and which is now being practised by many growers throughout Canada is briefly as follows: The new beginner first decides upon the variety with which to work. Where there are a number of different varieties in the district, he is advised to compare in small plots at least two or three varieties which seem to be giving good results. We also urge him to include the variety which is most highly recommended by his nearest experimental station. In most cases it is likely that the latter variety will be the one chosen since it will have been recommended because of its ability to give good results over a comparatively wide area and is therefore likely to be most in demand

POTATO YIELDS.

DIAGRAMS SHOWING VARIATION IN YIELD OF INDIVIDUAL ROWS OF POTATOES GROWN ON SPECIAL SEED PLOTS IN 1909:

CARMAN NO. I—(BY R. H. CROSBY, MARKHAM, ONT.)

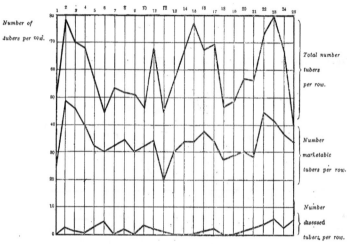

EMPIRE STATE—(BY R. H. CROSEY, MARKHAM, ONT.)

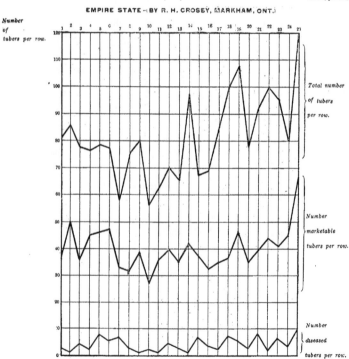

by the buying public. The choice of variety having been made, a quantity of the very best available seed of this variety is obtained to sow a special patch of land. Sometimes a grower obtains seed enough to plant all of the land he is devoting to potatoes. From the crop produced at least 25 or 30 of the best hills are selected and preserved for planting the following spring. During the first two or three years of his work, the grower is advised to keep the selected hills separate in paper sugar sacks or by means of some other convenient device, and plant these in separate rows or groups by themselves the following year. At dig-

careful work, or perhaps less where the grower starts with particularly good stock, the potatoes produced on this special patch may attain such a degree of purity and quality as to entitle them to be ranked as what the Association calls "Elite Stock Seed." This is the highest class of seed obtainable. The progeny of Elite Stock Seed up to and including three generations descended therefrom may be ranked as "Registered Seed." This is the class of seed which is offered for sale for seeding purposes.

SEED POTATO CENTRES

Owing to the fact that the type,

HAND-SELECTED SEED PLOT OF IRISH COBBLER POTATOES

ging time these different groups are kept by themselves in such a way that the grower may be able to select first the best groups, and then the best hills within each selected group. The accompanying illustration shows one of these seed plots which has just been dug by one of our growers.

After the first two or three years it is not quite so necessary to keep the selected hills separate, as these may be bulked together and planted on a special patch the following year. After two or three years'

in the case of potatoes, may be changed considerably by continuous selection, the Association considers it an unsafe practice, where the production of considerable quantities of a uniform type in a given district is desired, to have more than one man in such district do selection work. In order therefore to facilitate the production of quantities of uniform high class seed potatoes, the Association seeks to encourage the organization of what is known as "Seed Potato Centres." These centres consist of groups of growers in districts which are believed to be particularly suitable for the production of high class seed potatoes and who organize themselves into a definite body with responsible officers. Each centre chooses one of its number to produce first generation registered seed with which to supply the other growers and thus to obviate the necessity of each individual grower producing this class of seed himself. By obtaining a sack or two of first generation seed each spring and multiplying this for one year the members of a centre are able to have enough second generation seed to plant all of their potato land from

general product offered for sale may be vouched for, not only as regards its freedom from disease but as regards its productive capacity and trueness to type. Those who have to buy seed potatoes from year to year should find in these centres a reliable source of supply. The growers composing these groups should likewise find their work correspondingly remunerative.

INSPECTION OF SEED POTATOES

All seed potatoes grown for registration are inspected twice. The first inspection is made when the crop

A SEED POTATO PLOT PRODUCING "ELITE STOCK SEED"

year to year. The crop produced from this seed may be accepted for registration as third generation registered seed, providing it is up to standard as regards quality and freedom from disease. All seed complying with the standard set by the Association is advertised and handled by the centre as such rather than by the individual member thereof. This system, while quite new as applied to potatoes, bids fair to revolutionize the production of really first-class seed potatoes. By means of this system the purity of the stocks may be insured and the

is growing. At this time the purity of the variety, and the vigour and uniformity of growth, can be ascertained best. The second inspection considers the potatoes when they are dug, and takes into account the uniformity of type, quality, and freedom from disease. The inspection for disease is made under the supervision of the Dominion Botanist of the Dominion Experimental Farms. All potatoes which comply with the standards set by the Association regarding purity of type, uniformity, quality and freedom from disease are sealed in sacks or barrels with metal seals bearing the name of the Association. This seal is placed over a tag which bears the certificate number and also the signatures of the inspectors as well as of the grower, so that buyers ob-taining this seed may safely rely upon it. All registered seed potatoes, as well as seed of other crops, is given publicity in the seed catalogue issued by the Association, and distributed widely each spring.

POTATO GROWING CONTEST IN MANITOBA

THE following is taken from Bulletin No. 15, of the Manitoba Agricultural College, entitled "Manitoba Boys' and Girls' Clubs:

The contest in potato growing will be work with a well-known and desirable variety.

The potato originated in America and has grown to be one of the most important of food plants. The potato is eaten the world over more than any other crop except rice. It is grown very extensively now as a garden vegetable, as a truck crop, and in many sections of the country as a valuable field crop. Although the potato is adapted to a wide territory, certain varieties are best suited to particular climates and soils. Hence in selecting varieties special attention will be given to locality and soil texture.

RULES FOR POTATO GROWING CONTEST

1. Every member of each local branch of the Club will be supplied with ten pounds of a desirable variety of pure bred potatoes.

2. All potatoes must be planted and instructions must be followed as closely as possible.

3. Notes must be kept as outlined in paragraph on "note book," from which a composition of not more than two hundred words is to be prepared, giving the history of growing the crop. Credit will be given for this composition in placing the awards at the Fair.

4. From the note book each member must prepare a financial statement showing value of time expended in growing the crop.

5. In order that all competitors may have a uniform charge for labour, etc., the following schedule of rates is given and this members are expected to use:

1. Value of work for 1 horse, per hour $ .10
2. Value of work for two-horse team, per hour...................... .20
3. Value of work of contestant, per hour........................... .15
4. Value of each load of manure ... 1.00
5. Other expenses at actual cost.

6. Each member must exhibit at the club fair, one bushel of selected potatoes from the crop grown.

7. The "marketable" must be separated from the "unmarketable" potatoes and each weighed, and weight of each recorded in the financial statement.

8. The following score card will be used in placing the awards:

	Points.
1. Value of basis of yield...........	35
2. Quality as shown by exhibit of one bushel.....................	40
3. Written history of growing the crop (not more than 200 words)...	15
4. Financial statement showing value of labour expended in growing the crop..................	10

INSTRUCTIONS FOR POTATO GROWING

Choosing the Plot.—A light, sandy, loam soil is generally the best for potatoes. Avoid a heavy, wet, or cold soil. The potato partakes to a great extent of the soil in which it grows. However, much can be done in preparation of soil and in cultivation to overcome some conditions which are not favourable. Do not select soil where potatoes were grown the previous year. This will avoid scab and other diseases left by last year's crop. It is advisable to plant in long rows so that a horse cultivator may be used.

Preparation of Soil.—Prepare the soil well to make a mellow and fertile seed-bed. Treat land with well-rotted barnyard manure; plough deeply and then harrow and disc it until a good deep, fine, mellow seed-bed, free from trash, is made. This will provide just what the potato needs for a good start, and a good finish too.

Selecting Seed Potatoes.—Plant only good, healthy, well-shaped potatoes. The slightly flattened, oval shape, shallow-eyed, form of potato is preferred. They should be free from scab or other diseased condition and should have a healthy appearance. Strong seed helps to make strong plants and strong plants are necessary to get good yields.

Cutting Seed Potatoes.—The best size piece cuttings is a question that has not been definitely settled. When seed potatoes are very high in price it generally pays to make the smaller cuttings. Two good eyes to the seed piece, or good-sized potatoes cut into fourths, divided according to location of eyes, are the general rules under ordinary price conditions.

Planting.—Potatoes should be planted from three to four inches deep, according to soil and weather conditions. Usually it is advisable to plant potatoes between May 9th and 24th. If the plot is to be cultivated with a horse cultivator, the rows should be planted from three to three and one-half feet apart and of reasonable length. If in a rich garden plot and cultivation is to be done by hand, the rows may be planted closer and in hills in the row instead of in a continuous row as they would be if planted with a plough. In planting small samples it is advisable to plant with a hoe and press the soil down firmly with the hoe or the feet, while for field work the plough or potato planter is satisfactory. When in a continuous row a set should be dropped every twelve or fifteen inches. It is a slight advantage to place the set with the cut side down.

Cultivation.—The principal part of the cultivation should be done before the potatoes are planted. If the seed-bed has been properly prepared before planting, cultivation is then required only to keep the weeds out and the soil mellow and free from

crust on top. Harrowing until the potatoes come up will generally keep the weeds down, and the top soil mellow. The first cultivation may be quite deep if necessary to loosen the soil or to cover weeds, but, following this, care must be observed to prevent injury to the potato plant roots which spread from the rows. The frequency of cultivation depends largely upon the season. When the ground dries off after a rain and leaves a crust, the soil should be stirred as soon as it can be worked well. Weeds should be destroyed whenever they appear.

Spraying.—Watch for the potato beetle or "bug" as we sometimes call him. Do not let him get the start of you. Fight him with Paris green. It pays to spray potatoes. Do not wait until the potato beetles have large families to feed on your plants. Meet them early and as often as necessary to keep your potatoes free from the effects of their greedy appetites and from later visits of their extensive families.

Harvesting.—Wait until your potatoes are fully ripe. Harvest any time before frosty weather and when the soil is dry enough to handle well. Separate the "marketable" from the "unmarketable" potatoes, and find the exact weight of each. Store potatoes in a cool, dry place, and be prepared to exhibit one bushel at the Fall Club fair.

PRODUCTION OF POTATOES

From Agricultural War Book.

Countries.	1914 Bushels.	1913 Bushels.	1912 Bushels.
Great Britain and Ireland	272,516,000	283,913,000	213,783,000
France	....	477,115,000	552,074,000
Russia-in-Europe	....	1,274,452,000	1,356,824,000
Russia-in-Asia	....	32,622,000	58,564,000
Belgium	....	117,614,000	100,000,000
Serbia	....	....	2,154,000
Germany	1,680,000,000(a)	1,988,611,000	1,844,863,000
Austria	....	424,498,000⎫	686,307,000
Hungary	....	179,135,000⎭	
Italy	62,464,000	65,742,000	56,313,000
Denmark	28,551,000	39,306,000	28,889,000
Holland	....	91,958,000	121,878,000
Norway	....	25,876,000	29,825,000
Sweden	57,642,000	75,368,000	65,765,000
Canada	85,672,000	78,544,000	84,885,000
United States	450,921,000	331,525,000	420,647,000

Totals for 7 countries reported in 1914... 2,637,766,000 2,863,009,000 2,715,145,000

(a) From Broomhall's Corn Trade News.

NOTE—The production of potatoes in 7 countries in 1914 was 225,243,000 bushels less than in the same countries in 1913 and 77,379,000 bushels less than in 1912.

CULTIVATION OF VACANT LOTS

A PRACTICAL DEMONSTRATION FROM PHILADELPHIA.

PROBABLY no city in America has made such a practical success of the cultivation of vacant lots as Philadelphia. As a pioneer in the work the great Pennsylvanian City has had many imitators, including Boston, Buffalo, Detroit, Chicago, Rochester, N. Y., Worcester, Mass., all of which have had a measure of success and all of which have rendered a large amount of service to poor people. This is the nineteenth year of the operation of the system in Philadelphia. It is managed by a number of philanthropists under the title of the Vacant Lots' Cultivation Association with the assist-

education and recreation for thousands of men, women and children.

"Each one dollar makes four dollars and more on vacant lot gardens" is the inscription on the cover of the eighteenth annual report, which, under the title, "Our Method", says:

"We prepare the idle land, which is loaned to us, for cultivation by ploughing, harrowing, etc., then divide it into gardens about one-sixth of an acre in size and assign them to the families whose applications have been received.

"Fertilizer and sufficient good seed to

A BACK YARD GARDEN IN EARLY SPRING

ance of a superintendent and assistant superintendent, who alone receive remuneration. The work is mainly carried on by public subscriptions, which in 1914 amounted to $7,193, backed by the goodwill of the civic officials and the citizens generally. In this way the association has kept moving, although to-day it stands in debt $2,000, which is a little more than an average loss per year of a trifle above $100. Some twenty-five citizens loaned land last year, on which 603 gardens were created that produced thirty-two thousand dollars worth of crops besides providing better living for hundreds of families and increased health,

insure a successful start are furnished to the gardeners. Improved methods of gardening are shown.

"We charge the families nothing for the opportunity to cultivate these gardens, as the idle land is loaned to us without cost. The ploughing, fertilizer, seeds, etc., which we furnish to the families cost the association about $50 per garden. For these we charge $1 the first season, $2 the second season and so on, so that such families who continue to cultivate the garden the fifth season pay about the full cost of that which the Association furnishes to them.

"The families spread the fertilizer, plant the seeds, cultivate the growing crops and gather the matured produce. After supplying their family needs, they sell any surplus that remains.

"While acquiring health and happiness, and receiving valuable training and ex-. perience, the men, women and children join in increasing their material supplies. As their own work produces the results, they are not pauperized but encouraged to be more industrious and self-dependent, and acquire greater ability and self-respect."

there were five who gave a hundred dollars apiece, two five hundred each, and one, the president of the association, Samuel S. Fels, $1,000. They are all well repaid for their generosity by the fact that many otherwise almost impoverished families, add from 25 to 50 per cent to their scanty wages. A significant remark in one of the annual reports is, "Our work has been of great service to tubercular persons."

"The work", says another report, "has an important sociological value, since it has clearly pointed out a practical solution of the vexed problem of what shall be done

A BACK YARD GARDEN IN AUGUST

In the reports many interesting incidents are quoted illustrative of the work. A man of 82, for instance, won the first prize at the Vacant Lot Garden Exhibition at a Farmers' picnic; twelve gardens were cultivated by widows and a like number by cripples and men around four-score years of age. Of the 600 families thus assisted last year, 447 were of the labouring class or short time workers, while others had ill-health to contend with. The subscribers numbered nearly five hundred, the majority donating from $1 to $25, although

with the congested masses in the slums of our cities. The successful cultivation of vacant city lots has demonstrated that 'back to the farm' is no meaningless cry; that mother earth is ever ready to give to those who trust her a bountiful supply of food; that the cultivation of the soil gives not only sustenance for the body but bounding health, freedom of action and clearer vision. Every step taken to in_ duce a man to remain on the farm, or to return to the farm is a distinct contribution to the welfare of our country."

No better work can be done this year by any Board of Trade than that of assisting and fostering the food producing industries surrounding their town or city. They will be doing work profitable to themselves and to their country and the year 1915 should see the greatest production in the history of the Province.—*Honorary President Young in the Board of Trade News, Toronto, for March.*

MILKING REGULATIONS

T HE following are the Rules for Milkers" or "Milking Regulations" as displayed in the dairy stables of Government and Agricultural Educational Institutions:

AGRICULTURAL COLLEGE, TRURO

Professor John M. Trueman writes to THE GAZETTE:—

"We have no rules for the guidance of milkers posted in the college stable. Our regulations require the men to wear white suits, use a small top milking pail, wipe the cow's udder with a damp cloth, and milk with dry hands."

SCHOOL OF AGRICULTURE OF STE. ANNE DE LA POCATIÈRE

1. Treat the cows with the utmost kindness. Never shout or speak roughly.
2. Clean the cows, at least fifteen minutes before milking.
3. Clean the udder and the flank of the cow before milking.
4. Have your hands very clean.
5. Milk rapidly and completely.
6. Milk with dry hands.
7. Keep silent while milking.

OKA AGRICULTURAL INSTITUTE

1. Keep the stable always clean.
2. Avoid distributing dry fodder to the cattle or straw bedding while milking is in progress.
3. When milking is done outdoors, keep at a good distance from manure piles and infected places.
4. Wash your hands carefully and keep them absolutely clean.
5. Tie the cow's tail to her leg.
6. Wash the udder with lukewarm water and boracic acid.
7. Pass the sponge under the belly and the flake of the cow to gather loose hair and dust.
8. Wipe the udder with a clean cloth.
9. Milk in absolutely clean pails.
10. Use tin pails with a cover or a narrow opening.
11. Throw out the first four or five streams of milk.
12. Milk diagonally or crosswise.
13. Avoid anything that might disturb the cows. Keep them as quiet as possible.

14. Never strike or ill-treat your cows; kind treatment must always be the rule for dairy cows.
15. Milk with the full hand, and with dry hands.
16. Strip the udder completely.
17. Milk quickly; slow milking reduces the quantity of milk secreted.
18. Do not let the stable become cold when milking is being done; cold induces the cows to keep their milk.
19. Strain the milk as soon as it is milked, by passing it through a double cheese cloth.
20. In summer, cool the milk without aeration at about 50° F., and at a sufficient distance from the stables.
21. Milk at regular hours and at regular intervals. Any change in the time of milking always reduces the yield.
22. Always milk the same cows, and always in the same order.
23. Always wear a clean suit of clothes.

MACDONALD COLLEGE

1. Cows, if outside, must be tied in quietly, and with as little confusion as possible.
2. All manure must be scraped into gutters, care being taken to cause little disturbance of litter and dust in stable.
3. Milkers must wash their hands and face, comb their hair and put on milk suits.
4. Cans must be placed in dairy, strainers adjusted, separator set up, etc.
5. Each milker must provide himself with a wash cloth, and wash his hands and cloth in luke warm water after each milking. Cow's flanks, udders, teats, tails, etc., must be brushed off carefully, and then the teats and udder wiped with a damp cloth, *not washed.*
6. Each milker must be careful to do everything with the utmost cleanliness, keep his suit in as good condition as possible, avoid handling any part of the cow except her udder and teats, and to keep his pail in good condition.
7. Milking must be done rapidly and quietly , no noise such as yelling, whistling or talking will be tolerated in the stable.
8. Each milking must be weighed separately and recorded for the particular cow, then emptied into the receiving can in the dairy.

9. Each milker must watch for abnormal milk, such as bloody milk, swelled quarter, or any other such trouble and report at once to the man in charge.

10. In so far as is possible each man must milk the same cows, each time, and at the same hour, night and morning.

11. After all cows have been milked, the cows, if turned out, must be treated in the same way as when put in. The stable must be cleaned at once, and put in perfect condition.

12. Milk must be attended to as directed.

THE DOMINION EXPERIMENTAL FARMS

COW BARN GENERAL RULES

1. NO SMOKING IN BARNS: Visitors persisting in smoking in barns after request not to do so, shall be turned out of buildings. Employees breaking this rule shall be dismissed at once.

2. EVERY MAN TO BE ON TIME:

3. Men to obey orders promptly and follow rules exactly: any neglect or difficulties in these matters to be reported to the Animal Husbandman at once.

4. Stables to be cleaned twice a day: 7.30 in the morning; 2.30 in the afternoon.

5. Calf pens and box stalls to be cleaned every second day.

6. Windows, walls, etc., to be kept clean.

7. Iron work and wooden fixtures to be dusted or wiped with damp cloths once a week or more frequently, if necessary.

8. Manure to be wheeled to centre of yard. Any manure scattered along track to be gathered up and placed on the main pile.

9. Barrows, forks and shovels to be kept clean and in place.

10. Shovels to be used for distributing feed truck to manger.

11. Trucks and all other implements to be handled carefully and kept in good running order.

TIME TABLE

1. *Hours of Work:*
Begin work: 5.30 a.m.
Breakfast: 8.00 to 8.30.
Dinner: 12.00 to 1.00.
Stop Work: 5.30 to 5.45.

2. *Time Table:*
5.30 A. M. Preparation.
5.45 " Milking.
7.30 " Feeding and cleaning barn.
8.00 " Breakfast.
8.30 " Finish feeding-bedding.
9.00 " Sweeping and cleaning.
9.45 " Grooming and washing cows.
11.15 " Preparing feed.
12.00 " Noon Lunch.
1.00 P.M. Preparing. Feed–Odd jobs.
2.30 " Feeding and cleaning barn.
3.30 " Milking.
5.00 " Feeding and Sweeping.

MILKING RULES

In milking the following rules must be observed:

(a) Cows to be bedded down, at least 30 minutes before milking.

(b) Cows to be brushed, at least 20 minutes before milking.

(c) Udders and flanks to be brushed off with clean damp cloth, just before milking.

(d) Milker to wear jacket and apron These must be kept clean. Change three or more times per week, if necessary.

(e) Sleeves to be rolled up clear of wrist while milking, but shirt not to be exposed.

(f) Hands and face to be washed before beginning to milk.

(g) Towels must be kept clean and changed each day.

(h) Hands to be washed after milking each cow.

(i) No milk to be used on hands while milking. Vaseline may be used if desired.

(j) No unnecessary talking while milking.

(k) No tobacco chewing while milking.

(l) Cows to be treated kindly.

(m) Cows to be milked quickly, gently and thoroughly that is, clean out.

(n) Herdsman will direct men as to what cows they are to milk.

(o) Carelessness in brushing, wiping or milking shall be reported to the Animal Husbandman at once.

FINANCIAL ASSISTANCE TO AGRICULTURE

THE Jewish Agricultural and Industrial Aid Society, with headquarters in New York City, made in 1914, 327 loans to farmers amounting in all to $170,811.92. During the year they received in the way of repayments from farmers a total of $124,786.37. Of this amount $93,022.05 was principal and $31,764.32 interest. In fifteen years this society has granted a total of 3,318 loans to farmers aggregating $1,910,227.68. These loans were made to 2,876 farmers occupying 2,387 individual farms in thirty-four states and the Dominion of Canada.

This society in 1914 placed 934 men in positions as farm labourers. The total cost of conducting the Farm Labour Bureau of the society for the year was $1,243.71. The society issues a monthly magazine called the "Jewish Farmer" which is printed in the English and Hebrew languages.

The society organized an educational staff which delivers lectures on agricultural subjects in various farming communities, at farmers' institutes and farmers' demonstration meetings and pays personal visits to individual farmers. The society also grants free scholarships to children of poor farmers to enable them to pursue the short courses of agriculture offered by the Agricultural Colleges of their respective states. One hundred and seventeen of these scholarships have been provided at an average cost of $92.29 per scholarship. With few exceptions, those who have taken scholarships are said to be working on the home farms. The association encourages organization and co-operation among its members. Beginning in 1909, with nineteen associations, it had, at the end of 1914, sixty-three with a total membership of 1178. These are organized solely for agricultural purposes. The federation of societies includes the Co-operative Purchasing Bureau, Credit Unions, Co-operative Fire Insurance, Co-operative Creameries and other Co-operative enterprises.

CO-OPERATIVE EXPERIMENTS IN WEED ERADICATION

DURING the past three years, 1912-13-14, the Ontario Agricultural and Experimental Union, under the direction of J. E. Howitt, M. S. A., Professor of Botany at the Ontario Agricultural College, carried on co-operative experiments in the eradication of weeds. Some forty-five farmers co-operated in this work. The weeds experimented with were Perennial Sow Thistle, Twitch Grass, Bladder Campion, Wild Mustard and Ox-eye Daisy. Some very interesting and valuable results were obtained. Those who took part in these experiments profited by the experience. In nearly every instance they cleaned the field experimented with, and demonstrated to their own satisfaction the effectiveness of the method tried, and at the same time their results furnished practical information to others.

These co-operative weed experiments will be continued this year (1915). The weeds to be experimented with are Perennial Sow Thistle, Twitch Grass, Bladder Campion or Cow Bell, Wild Mustard and Ox-eye Daisy.

LIST OF EXPERIMENTS IN WEED ERADICATION

1. The use of rape in the destruction of Perennial Sow Thistle.
2. A system of intensive cropping and cultivation, using winter rye followed by turnips, rape or buckwheat, for eradicating Perennial Sow Thistle.
3. The use of rape in the destruction of Twitch Grass.
4. Method for the eradication of Bladder Campion or Cow Bell.

5. Spraying with iron sulphate to destroy mustard in cereal crops.
6. A method of cultivation for the destruction of Ox-eye Daisy.

SOME OF THE PRACTICAL INFORMATION GAINED FROM THESE CO-OPERATIVE WEED EXPERIMENTS

1. That good cultivation, followed by rape sown in drills, provides a means of eradicating both Perennial Sow Thistle and Twitch Grass.
2. That rape is a more satisfactory crop to use in the destruction of Twitch Grass than buckwheat.
3. That rape gives much better results in the eradication of Twitch Grass and Perennial Sow Thistle when sown in drills and cultivated than it does when sown broadcast.
4. That thorough deep cultivation in fall and spring followed by a well cared for hoed crop will destroy Bladder Campion.
5. That mustard may be prevented from seeding in oats, wheat and barley by spraying with a twenty per cent solution of iron sulphate without any serious injury to the standing crop or to the fresh seedings of clover.

REGARDING EXPERIMENTS

The object of these experiments is to gather data from which definite statements may be made regarding the best methods of controlling the various bad weeds. It is hoped to include more weeds each year until exact information has been obtained about the eradication of most of the bad weeds of Ontario.

CLASSES FOR THE STUDY OF BIRDS

THE National Association of Audubon Societies, with headquarters at 1974 Broadway, New York City, offers assistance to those teachers, and others who are interested in giving instruction to children on the subject of birds and their usefulness. The offer involves, among other things, the forming of Junior Audubon Classes. Last year the pupils engaged in these classes numbered more than 115,000 and represented every State in the Union and several provinces in Canada.

The Association or State Society will then forward to the teachers for each member whose fee has been paid, a beautiful Audubon button, and a set of ten coloured picture of birds, the list of which is changed every year; and with them will go outline drawings, suitable for colouring by the children, and descriptive leaflets. The teacher reporting the class will also receive free of cost, for one year, the finely illustrated magazine *Bird–Lore*, which contains many valuable suggestions for teachers. Should the class then, or subsequently, be enlarged, a button and a set of leaflets will be added for each new member until the end of the school year. In return, it is expected that the teacher shall give at least one lesson a month on the subject of birds, and that the leaflets shall serve as a basis for the lessons, but experience shows that usually much more than this is done.

Full information as to the details of this plan, and a simple form of organization for a class, may be had by addressing a request to the National Association. The list of ten birds to be studied this year includes the brown thrasher, nut-hatch, bluebird, downy woodpecker, Baltimore oriole, robin, bobolink, goldfinch, song sparrow and green heron.

BY-LAWS FOR AUDUBON CLASS

If the teacher wishes, the Audubon class may have a regular organization, and a pupil may preside upon the occasions when the class is discussing a lesson. For this purpose the following simple set of by-laws is suggested:

ARTICLE I. This organization shall be known as the Junior Audubon class.

ARTICLE II. The objects of its members shall be to learn all they can about the wild birds, and to try to save any from being wantonly killed.

ARTICLE III. The officers shall consist of a President, Secretary and Treasurer.

ARTICLE IV. The annual fees of the class shall consist of 10 cents for each member; and the money shall be sent to the National Association of Audubon societies in exchange for educational leaflets and Audubon buttons.

ARTICLE V. The Junior Audubon class shall have at least one meeting every month.

Although most of these classes have been and will be formed among pupils in schools, any one may form a class of children anywhere, and receive the privileges offered.

CO-OPERATIVE WOOL MARKETING IN SASKATCHEWAN

IN the past wool production in Saskatchewan has not brought in as large returns as it should. This is partially due to the lack of proper care in preparing the fleeces for market; and also to the fact that usually the wool was sold in small quantities and had to be shipped long distances in less than car lots. To overcome these defects in our wool marketing system, the Provincial Department of Agriculture, through the Co-operative Organization branch, last spring undertook, without charge, to market the clip for sheep men who would prepare their wool in accordance with directions drawn up by the department. Some 180 sheep owners took advantage of this offer, a total of 69,404 pounds of wool was assembled in a warehouse in Regina, and sold in car lots to a firm of American wool dealers, an average price of 16.47 cents being paid to the producers after defraying all cost for freight to Regina, cost of sacks, twine, and other incidental expenses. Considering that prices received in former years ranged from 10 cents to 13 cents per pound, the results were most satisfactory.

To further stimulate the sheep raising industry in the province the department again intends carrying on this work. This season, in addition to operating a receiving and grading warehouse in Regina, arrangements are being made to accept delivery of car-load lots of wool at any local shipping point in the province. This arrangement should add materially to the value of the undertaking as there are many points where three or four breeders could combine to make up a car lot, thereby increasing prices by reducing freight charges.

HOME ECONOMICS IN MANITOBA

IN the last report of the Department of Agriculture of Manitoba, Mrs. C. Charlton Salisbury, furnishes a most encouraging account of the work of the Home Economics societies in Manitoba. Nine new societies and several hundred new members were added last year, bringing the membership up to 1,675. Much useful work has been done in placing unemployed girls, in introducing social improvements, in the creation and care of beauty spots in localities, and above all in making articles of comfort for the refugee and the wounded. The societies in fact have been very generally employed in Red Cross work.

The Provincial Department of Agriculture helps along by a grant of 50 cents for each member up to twenty in number and 25 cents for every additional member. The Department last year also contributed 240 books to the travelling libraries of the societies. Four of these libraries exist, each of which contains from twelve to fifteen books on Home Economics, which are kept in constant circulation between the different societies. Finally, Mrs. Salisbury says that progress is being made not only in educational work but in everything looking to the improvement of home and community conditions.

AGRICULTURE IN RURAL SCHOOLS

THE Better Farming committee of the Canadian Credit Men's Association, after listening to an address by Mayor Waugh of Winnipeg on "Farming First", adopted the following resolutions approving of the steps now being taken by the governments of the three prairie provinces to introduce a course of practical agriculture in rural schools.

TRAINING IN RURAL SCHOOLS

"Resolved, that this association, recognizing the development of agricultural efficiency is being furthered in other countries by the inclusion of an agricultural course in their school systems, heartily approves of the steps now being taken by the governments of the three prairie provinces, to introduce a course of practical agricultural instruction in our rural schools, and urge that no time be lost in carrying this policy to completion."

FARM KNOWLEDGE FOR THE CITY BOY.

"Also resolved, that as in the opinion of this association, it is desirable to encourage

an interest in agriculture on the part of children dwelling in cities, and to develop latent agricultural talent wherever it exists among city boys and girls, the Minister of Education for Manitoba and the Winnipeg Public School Board be requested to consider the advisability of establishing one or more primary schools adjacent to the city for the purpose of providing a practical course in agriculture."

TO MAKE AGRICULTURAL COLLEGE MORE ACCESSIBLE

"Further resolved, that with a view to facilitate any tendency on the part of the city boys to take up the pursuit of farming, the Departments of Agriculture for each of the Central Western provinces be urged to modify the regulation of the Agricultural College so as to allow boys residing in cities or towns to be entered as students after having been engaged in farm employment for a period of six consecutive months, their continuance at the college for a second year to be conditional, if thought necessary, on their spending a further six months on a farm."

COUNTY AGENT EARNS $410,000

SCOTT county, Iowa, has had a county agent for two years. In those two years this county estimates that the net cash value of crops increased, animals saved and profits from silos built, is $410,500.

When Scott county decided that it was ripe for a county agent, a Davenport

banker was persuaded to become president of the county organization, known as the Farm Improvement league. He has served as its leader for two years, and has given much time to the work.

Two years ago there were 146 acres of alfalfa in the county; now there are 1,086. The increased cash value was figured on actual production, and the figures are for the value of the crop above timothy and clover.

The increase in. corn is computed from the records of early gathering and testing of seed. Scott county farmers were well in the lead on proper selection and testing of seed corn before organized work began, but seed selection has greatly increased. In 1912, 43,000 acres were planted with such seed. This increased to 60,000 acres in 1913 and 56,000 acres were planted in 1914. State authorities estimate five bushels per acre as the increased yield from such planting, but wishing to be conservative, the figures in this table are based on an increase of only two bushels per acre, valued at 50c per bushel.

The gain in oats is the result of the campaigns for the treatment of seed for smut, and the increased yields are taken from careful returns received. In 1912 but 1,100 acres of oats were sown with treated seed;. while in 1913, it had increased to 4,400 acres, and in 1914 it was 11,220 acres. The figures on silos are based on an estimated profit of $200 per silo.

The league conducted experiments in serum treatment for hog-cholera, which demonstrated its efficacy. As a result, 17,420 hogs were treated in 1913, of which 14,284 (or 82 per cent.) were saved. In

1914, 18,611 hogs were treated, of which 16,377 (or 88 per cent.) were saved. The value of the hogs saved is placed at $10 per head, surely a conservative estimate.

"If to this splendid total of over $400,000 we could compute and add the direct cash value of other activities of this organized work, the sum would be considerably larger," said President Dawson in an address to farmers. "We have no accurate data to show how much the farmers have profited by the work of urging the treatment of seed barley for smut, or of potatoes for scab; in the spraying of orchards, and the varied experiments conducted on the experimental farm."

Net cash value to Scott county, Iowa, of crops increased, animals saved and profits from silos built after the county agent came:

Kind of work:	1913	1914
Alfalfa............$	3,500	$ 13,000
Corn..../..........	17,000	13,000
Oats..............	14,600	28,500
Silos..............	6,000	8,400
Hogs saved... ...	142,800	163,700
Totals......... ...	$183,900	$226,600
Total for two years		$410,500

From *The Banker-Farmer.*

COLLEGE EXTENSION WORK

The Extension Department of the West Virginia College of Agriculture announces the following results. accomplished in five counties of that State in 1914 through the agency of County Agricultural Agents:

SOIL IMPROVEMENT DEMONSTRATIONS.

Drainage........................(approx.)	539 acres tiled.
Lime............................ "	10,986 acres treated with lime.
Phosphorus... .... "	9,408 acres treated with ac. phosphate.
Manure......................... "	4,284 tons saved by extra care.
Legumes........................ "	2,205 acres to be turned under.
Other cover crops.... . ... "	6,163 acres to be turned under.

FIELD CROP DEMONSTRATIONS.

Corn...	987 acres at average of 51 bu. against county average, 25 bu.
Potatoes....	198 acres at average of 81 bu. against county average, 45 bu.
Orchard crops. :.......	53,100 trees given attention.
Alfalfa...............	697 acres harvested.
Alfalfa...............	1,070 acres seeded.
Cowpeas and soy beans..	761 acres harvested for hay or seed.

LIVE STOCK DEMONSTRATIONS.

Silos.............'......................	302 filled for first time.
Pastures............	915 acres treated.
Pure bred sires... .:..............	80 introduced.
Dairy cows.........................	171 under test by scales and Babcock tester.
Cattle and cows... :...............	4,604 fed modified economical rations.
Poultry...........................	187 poultry houses remodeled.

Of 1,404 well hogs treated with cholera serum—saved.... ....96 per cent.
Of 946 sick hogs treated with cholera serum—saved ....73 " "

SOCIETIES AND ASSOCIATIONS.

PRINCE EDWARD ISLAND POULTRY ASSOCIATION

At the annual meeting of the Prince Edward Island Poultry Association, March, 1915, the following officers were elected:

Honorary Presidents: His Hon. Lieut.-Governor Rogers; Hon. Murdock Mc-Kinnon, Commissioner of Agriculture. President, R. V. Longworth, Charlotte-town; vice-president for Queen's county, Henry Lapthorne; vice-president for Prince county, Vernon Matthew; vice-president, for King's county, Richard Murley. Directors: A. F. Houston, W. J. Cudmore, Arthur Nelson, Robert Haynes; superintendent, John Whitlock; secretary-treasurer, Geo. Lightizer, Charlottetown.

In a letter to THE AGRICULTURAL GAZETTE, Mr. George Lightizer, the Secretary, says:

"The Association has recently been taking a very special interest in the utility Department of Poultry, and it is hoped that this will encourage our farmers in the production of more and better poultry and eggs. The Federal Department of Agriculture has greatly assisted us in the matter of the expenses in connection with providing for competent judges, and our Provincial Department of Agriculture has rendered us valuable support in many ways, including the equipping of the Agricultural Hall, Charlottetown, with a large number of up-to-date coops for the accommodation of the exhibits.

"This valuable assistance given by the two Departments of Agriculture has, we think, been very instrumental in making the Association a real benefit to the poultry industry of this province.

A prominent feature in connection with the poultry industry of the province is the reformation of methods of marketing eggs, due to the organization of what are known as egg circles. This organization has made wonderful advances during a little less than two years, and there are at present upwards of 60 local Co-operative Egg Marketing Associations in the province, all of which are affiliated to a Central Association incorporated by an Act of the Provincial Legislature. This work which was initiated by a resident representative of the Federal Department of Agriculture, by whom the movement has been organized and is being perfected with further assistance being rendered by the Federal and Provincial Departments of Agriculture, bids fair to firmly establish good methods of marketing and to greatly increase production. Increased production is already noticeable in districts where egg circles are in operation.

NEW BRUNSWICK FARMERS' AND DAIRYMEN'S ASSOCIATION

At the thirty-ninth annual session of the New Brunswick Farmers' and Dairymen's Association held at Sussex, N.B., on March 8, 9, 10 and 11, the following among other resolutions were passed:

Confidence in agricultural policy of Dominion and Province.

Recommendation to Provincial Department of Agriculture to effect an organization in each county of the province that will more closely bind together the agricultural interests of the respective counties.

A recommendation to vice-presidents to get in touch with the various agricultural societies in their counties with a view to co-operate in influencing their respective municipal councils to put in force a tax on dogs, said tax to be a fund from which owners of sheep killed by dogs may be reimbursed for losses incurred through the ravages of dogs.

A recommendation to vice-presidents to make every effort to get the agricultural societies in their respective counties to co-operate in influencing their municipal councils to enforce the law prohibiting scrub bulls running at large in sections where efforts have been made, and are being made, to introduce pure bred cattle.

The officers for the ensuing year were appointed as follows; President, J. T. Prescott, Sussex; vice-president, A. F. Dickson, Chatham; correspondent-secretary, A. R. Wetmore, Clifton; recording-secretary, C. M. Shaw, Hartland; treasurer, H. H. Smith, Hoyt Station.

SASKATCHEWAN VETERINARY ASSOCIATION

At the annual meeting of the association held in Regina in March the following officers were appointed:

President: Dr. C. Head, Regina; vice-president: Dr. H. Richards, Indian Head; secretary-treasurer and registrar: Dr. R. G. Chasmar, Hanley; executive committee: Dr. M. P. Mc-Lellan, Regina; Dr. Norman Wright, Saskatoon; Dr. A. G. Hopkins, Bratton.

BRITISH COLUMBIA FRUIT GROWERS' ASSOCIATION

Following are two of the more important resolutions passed by the British Columbia Fruit Growers' Association at their latest annual meeting:

Whereas the great growth of the fruit industry both in Canada and the United States has caused it to be more difficult to get profitable markets; and whereas it has been pretty well proved and is generally agreed that the cutting of prices, in order to obtain sales by agents, dealers, and others, including growers themselves, has greatly lessened the amount of money that might have been received for the fruit; and whereas the getting together of those handling fruit at least in some way that will keep prices from being unnecessarily lowered, to the ruin of the grower and injury of the whole population, is necessary: Be it therefore *Resolved*, That all Fruit-growers' Associations, Farmers' Institutes, Boards of Trade, business-men, newspapers, and the Government of the Province be asked to help create such a public sentiment that will demand that fruit be not slaughtered by unseemly competition. And be it further *Resolved*, That the British Columbia Fruit-growers' Association appoint a committee to seek to solve this problem and to help to bring together the heads of the various selling agencies.

(1.) *Resolved*, That in the interests of the fruit-growers there should be some means of procuring loans at a cheaper rate and on better terms than is possible under present conditions.

(2.) Whereas the rates of interest and the difficulties of obtaining loans place a great burden on farmers and fruit-growers in seeking to improve their lands; and whereas great improvement has been made and general prosperity promoted in countries that have made large loans, properly guarded, at low rates of interest to settlers; and whereas the Agricultural Commission has recommended a similar undertaking for this Province: Be it therefore *Resolved*, That we unite with other agricultural bodies in asking the Government as speedily as possible to arrange for loans to settlers at a low rate of interest, for improvements to farms, purchase of stock, etc., and that the funds should be administered by an impartial non-political Commission.

JUNIOR FARMERS' IMPROVEMENT ASSOCIATION.

A meeting of the members of the Five Weeks' Agricultural Course held in Brighton last year and of those who attended the six weeks' course at Warkworth this winter was held in the Agricultural Office, Brighton, Northumberland County, Ont., Saturday, March 13th.

Deep interest was manifested in the new organization, for forming which the meeting was called. This is known as the Junior Farmers' Improvement Association of Northumberland, the object of which is to organize the young men of the farms into a consolidated working body, who in co-operation with the district representative will conduct field crops and feeding competitions conduct various experiments either of their own choosing or those suggested by the Agricultural Department or the Ontario Agricultural College, to be a medium for the distribution of farm literature and to improve general farm conditions in their own locality. R. S. Beckett, District Representative, opened the meeting with a brief address emphasizing the importance of such an organization, after which the following officers were elected:—

President, Oscar Laver, Norham; vice-president, Arthur Down, Hilton; secretary-treasurer, Maurice Herrington, Hilton; directors, Arthur Brown, Warkworth, Harvie Wilton, Castleton; Garnet Hardy, Morganston; Raymond McGillis, Brighton; Donald McConnel, Brighton.

Two meetings of the association will be held yearly. The organization is limited to the members of the Agricultural Short Courses in the county, but will enlarge rapidly from year to year as the students of succeeding classes are added. As the course is held in a different centre each year, it is only the matter of a few years before the county will be covered and the whole of Northumberland will be represented in this enterprizing and promising association.

GOOD ROADS ASSOCIATION

At a business session of the Canadian Good Roads' Association, held recently in Toronto, Mr. B. Michaud, deputy minister of roads for the province of Quebec, was elected president for the ensuing year. The meeting place of the congress for next year was not chosen. Other officers elected were: Honorary presidents, Messrs. W. A. McLean and H. H. Dandurand; secretary-treasurer, G. A. McNamee, Montreal; educational committee, Messrs. W. A. McLean. O. Hezzlewood, J. Duchastel, R. S. Henderson, P. J. Shore, Lieut.-Col. Ponton, J. A. Sanderson, W. Pillow and G. A. McNamee.

CATTLE BREEDERS' ASSOCIATION OF MANITOBA

The 12th annual sale of Pure Bred Bulls, held under the auspices of the Cattle Breeders' Association of Manitoba, on March 18th, in Brandon, was a decided success. The animals on the whole, were of fair quality, and brought in in respectable condition, many of them being in excellent shape. There was a notable absence of aged and thin animals. Entries were made by many of the prominent breeders of the province, as evidenced by the catalogue. The sale was conducted in the Brandon Winter Fair Building, T. Crawford Norris acting as auctioneer. The terms were cash, and every animal was settled for within an hour after the close of the sale, and shipped to the buyer's nearest station within 24 hours after the sale had closed. The averages made by the various breeds are as follows:—

		Average.
9 Angus Bulls	$1,345	$149.44
1 " Female	200	
2 Hereford Bulls	310	155.00
1 Holstein Bull	80	
43 Shorthorn Bulls	6,620	153.95
1 Shorthorn Female	75	
57	$8,630	$151.40

NORTH BATTLEFORD LIVE STOCK COMPANY

Continuing the reports of the organization and work of co-operative live stock associations commenced in the December number and continued in February, Commissioner F. Wright, of the North Battleford Board of Trade, sends particulars relating to the North Battleford Live Stock Company, Limited, a company founded by a former mayor of the town, who is still president. Mr. Wright defines the object of the company as: "To buy live stock on borrowed money and to sell to farmers on extended credit." In other words the company becomes surety for the farmer. The company, organized in 1913, is capitalized at $25,000, three-fourths of which has been subscribed. The shares are $10 each and purchasers of live stock from the company must each hold at least one share. A clause in the articles of incorporation prohibits the declaration of any dividend on the stock. Five per cent has been paid up, and the bank lends money on the total guaranteed subscriptions. At the meetings preliminary to organization, the founder, then Mayor Griese, F. W. Hodson, and others delivered addresses. Live Stock is sold on terms to suit the purchaser, who gives a mortgage covering the cost of the animals. He also gives a six months' note bearing interest at 8 per cent. If these notes cannot be met in whole at maturity the balance is renewed for another six months. If the purchaser needs it he can continue for a further six months, thus obtaining eighteen months in which to make repayment. When possible, arrangements are made with purchasers of milch cows to send cream to the North Battleford Creamery, for which credit is endorsed on the notes. Up to the end of March transactions covering $14,000, had

been completed, including the buying of 90 dairy cattle in Eastern Ontario. A small percentage is added to the cost of each animal to cover incidental expenses and to create a reserve fund for protection against losses. The clerical work is done by officials of the Board of Trade and the City Treasurer looks after the collections, so that no salary is paid outside that of a man at intervals to superintend the care of the animals on arrival. Commissioner Wright says that the scheme is an undoubted success and has proved a stimulus to the live stock industry.

LIVE STOCK ASSOCIATIONS OF SASKATCHEWAN

The various Live Stock Associations of Saskatchewan held their annual meetings at Regina on March 9, 10, 11—1915. Numerous resolutions dealing with matters of prime importance to stock breeders in the Western Provinces, were thoroughly discussed and a large number of them carried; amongst these were: "The dog and coyote menace to the sheep industry", "Bovine tuberculosis", The establishment of the chilled meat industry in the West", "Co-operative marketing of wool and live stock" and "The running at large of entire animals". Resolutions were also passed commending the distribution of cattle and co-operative marketing of wool by the Department of Agriculture, and also recognizing the suitability of the Provincial gift of military horses to the Imperial Government.

At these meetings the nucleus of at least two new organizations was formed—these were —a Provincial Co-operative Live Stock Marketing Association, and a Clydesdale Club.

The following are the officers of the associations elected for 1915:

SHEEP BREEDERS' ASSOCIATION

President, A. B. Potter, Langbank; vice-president, E. E. Baynton, Maple Creek; secretary-treasurer, J. Cochrane Smith, Regina; directors, W. C. Sutherland, Saskatoon; J. L. Beattie, Piapot; J. Browne, Neudorf.

HORSE BREEDERS' ASSOCIATION

President, R. H. Taber, Condie; vice-president, H. Gilmour, Pasqua; secretary-treasurer, J. Cochrane Smith, Regina; directors, R. W. Hamill, Regina; R. Sinton, Regina; W. C. Sutherland, Saskatoon; Alex. Mutch, Lumsden. Horse Breeders' Representative on Stallion Licensing Board.—W. H. Bryce, Arcola.

CLYDESDALE CLUB

After the meeting of the horse breeders, a meeting of Clydesdale breeders was held, and it was decided to form a provincial Clydesdale club for the purpose of advancing the interests and qualities of this breed. The officers elected were: President, R. H. Taber; vice-president, W. H. Bryce; secretary, D. T. Elderkin; directorate, H. Gilmour, W. C. Sutherland, Alex. Mutch.

SWINE BREEDERS' ASSOCIATION

Hon. President, F. T. Skinner, Indian Head; president, S. V. Tomecko, Lipton; vice-president, J. G. Robertson, Davidson; secretary-treasurer, J. Cochrane Smith, Regina; directors, C. G. Bulstrode, Qu'Appelle; A. B. Potter, Langbank; John Ames, Hanley.

CATTLE BREEDERS' ASSOCIATION

President, W. C. Sutherland; Saskatoon; vice-president, A. B. Potter, Langbank; directors: J. Barnett, Moose Jaw; J. Brandt, Edenwold; R. M. Douglas, Tantallon; secretary, J. C. Smith, Regina.

WINTER FAIR BOARD

The annual meeting of the Saskatchewan Winter Fair Board was held in Regina on March 11th, at which it was decided to hold the 1916 Fair either late in February or early in March.

It was further decided to widen the scope of the Winter Fair Board by combining it with the Provincial Live Stock Executive and a committee was appointed to draft a charter and draw up proposed alterations in the constitution.

A resolution was passed asking the railroads for a combined tariff on stock and market poultry shipped in the same car.

The formation of a Provincial Co-operative Live Stock Marketing Association was endorsed. It is hoped to hold Winter Fairs at both Regina and Saskatoon in 1916, and committees of management were selected for both places.

The following officers were elected for the year.—

President, Robert Sinton, Regina; vice-president, W. C. Sutherland, Saskatoon; secretary-treasurer, J. C. Smith, Regina.

The directorate consists of the presidents and vice-presidents of the provincial live stock associations.

SALE OF PURE BRED CATTLE

At the annual auction sale of pure bred cattle held under the auspices of the Saskatchewan Cattle Breeders' Association, 64 animals were exposed for sale, of which 48 sold at an average price of $131.00 per head.

The demand was not brisk and the fact that a number of the remaining animals changed hands after the sale on credit terms would indicate that the present financial stringency was partly responsible for this state of affairs.

Of the animals offered, 44 were Shorthorns, 6 Aberdeen Angus, 6 Herefords, 5 Holsteins and 3 Ayrshires.

BOOK REVIEWS

The Principles of Fruit Growing, by L. H. Bailey. The MacMillan Company, New York and Toronto, 5¼ by 7½ inches, 432 pages, illustrated.

This is the twentieth edition of a work that first came out in 1897, but it has been so completely re-arranged, and so largely re-written that it is to a great extent a new book. It belongs to the Rural Science Series. In recent years much new knowledge has come to the aid of the fruit grower. This relates to tillage, insect and fungous control, protection from frost, fertilization, packing, marketing, etc. The present edition embodies the most advanced ideas on these and various other phases of the industry, all of which are presented in plain language, aided in many cases by illustrations. As an indication of the exhaustive character of the work, it may be mentioned that the index to the volume requires the space of more than nine pages.

Plant Breeding, by L. H. Bailey, Professor of Horticulture in Cornell University, Ithaca, N. Y.; The MacMillan Co., London, New York and Toronto; 5 x 7½ inches, 483 pages; price $2.00.

This is the fourth edition of a work comprising six lectures upon "The Amelioration of Domestic Plants" by perhaps the best authority on horticulture in the United States. Mr. Bailey has written a great variety of books on plant life, but possibly none has attracted more attention and been more widely quoted than the present volume. To this edition has been added a valuable chapter on "Current Plant Breeding Practice." Professor Bailey is thorough in all he undertakes. In his preface he says very rightly "that one cannot understand the production of new varieties until he has grasped some of the fundamental principles of the onward progression of the vegetable kingdom. Any attempt, therefore, to explain the origin of garden varieties, and the methods of producing them, must be at the same time a contribution to the literature of the philosophy of organic evolution." In that quotation a key to the work is supplied. The first lecture deals with "The Fact and Philosophy of Variation"; the second with "The Philosophy of the Crossing of Plants, considered in reference to their Improvement under Cultivation"; the third, with "How Domestic Varieties Originate"; the fourth with "Recent Opinions, being a Résumé of the Investigation of De Vries, Mendel and others, and a Statement of the Current Tendencies of American Plant-Breeding Practice"; the fifth with "Current Plant-Breeding Practice" and the sixth with "Pollination, or How to Cross Plants".

Agriculture, Theoretical and Practical, by J. Wrightson and J. C. Newsham; London, Crosby Lockwood & Son.

While this is a work written entirely from an English point of view, it contains in its six hundred odd pages much of most valuable matter to the peoples of all countries. Right Hon., the Earl of Northbrook, who in a brief introduction pays tribute to the abilities as agriculturists of the authors, who indeed in their multifarious connections appear to be well ahead of their fellows, both in practical experience and as instructors, aptly sums up the scope of the volume when he says: "This book is eminently suggestive as to the best methods of applying science to practice. It lays stress upon many problems which are destined to produce far-reaching consequences on fertility, land cultivation and rural economy. The subjects treated are very numerous, and include not only cultivation, but such important matters as farm buildings, book-keeping and the relative merits of grass and arable land." The second title of the work is "A Textbook of Mixed Farming for Large and Small Farmers and for Agricultural Students." There are six parts, the first, divided into ten chapters, deals with Soils, Manures and Crops; the second, consisting of seven chapters, with Live Stock, Feeding and Economic Zoology; the third, of four chapters, with Buildings, Machinery, Implements and Accounts; the fourth, of three chapters, with Dairying; the fifth, of four chapters. with Horticulture, and the sixth, of three chapters, with Poultry, Rabbits and Bees. Numerous appropriate illustrations of bird, beast, plant life, insects and machinery lend great value to a book that at six shillings net in England must be accounted wonderfully cheap. Possibly it is in the live stock section. with its particular description of breeds of animals of all sorts, that the most value to Canadians will be found.

NEW PUBLICATIONS

THE DOMINION DEPARTMENT OF AGRICULTURE

EXPERIMENTAL FARMS SERIES

Lime in Agriculture. This is Bulletin No. 80 of the regular series of the Experimental Farms.

One of the principal functions of the chemical division of the Experimental Farms is to solve many of the problems that are connected with the maintaining and building up the fertility of the soil. Much work in this direction has already been accomplished. It has been ascertained by experiment that the part played by lime in maintaining and increasing fertility is an exceedingly great one. As to the quantities of lime-stone in the Dominion and for the information of farmers as to how and to what extent this may be used with advantage by farmers, a bulletin has been prepared by Dr. Frank T. Shutt, Dominion Chemist, dealing with this subject under the following heads:—

The nature of lime and lime-stone.

The agricultural functions of lime and its compounds.
Comparative value of lime compounds.
The appropriation of lime compounds.
The use and misuse of lime.

THE LIVE STOCK BRANCH

The Great Neglect in Sheep Husbandry is the title of Pamphlet No. 9 of the Sheep and Goat Division, for which T. Reg. Arkell and Norman Stansfield are responsible. It deals with castration and docking and points to the great necessity of these operations. Reasons are supplied and methods illustrated.

DIVISION OF HORTICULTURE

"*The Home Vegetable Garden and a Patriotic Gardening Competition.*" Pamphlet No. 13, Experimental Farms Series, by W. T. Macoun, Dominion Horticulturist. This pamphlet is especially timely, coming at a period when the attention of dwellers in towns and cities is being directed to the use they could make of back-yards, waste land and vacant lots.

The Dominion Horticulturist gives advice as to the situation of the garden, preparation of the soil, planning, seeds to sow, methods of cultivation, vegetables and plants that can be grown and so on. He also supplies rules and regulations that could be adopted by municipalities, fair associations and other organizations for patriotic vegetable gardening competitions.

PROVINCIAL DEPARTMENTS OF AGRICULTURE

ONTARIO

Pure Bred Live Stock Census of Peel. This pamphlet, compiled by the Peel County Branch of the Ontario Department of agriculture, gives information relative to the extent of the pure bred live stock industry in the county, and brings prominently before all interested parties the names of the breeders, together with the breeds, ages and number of animals in their possession. The information contained therein was obtained directly from breeders during the latter part of the year 1914, and in order to keep this information before the public it is intended that similar lists shall be tabulated and distributed annually.

Smuts and Rusts of Grain Crops.—This is Bulletin No. 229 of the Ontario Department of Agriculture, prepared by J. E. Howitt, M. S. A., Professor of Botany at the Ontario Agricultural College, and R. E. Stone, B. Sc., Ph. D., Lecturer in Botany. It is estimated that the losses sustained from smut in Ontario grain crops amount to $2,720,000 annually, but two-thirds of which occurs in oats, wheat being the next greatest sufferer. To cope with this danger this very practical bulletin goes fully into the cause and cure of smut and rusts and gives a number of ways of treating seed grain, in order to avoid or lessen injury to grain crops from these causes.

Farm Crops. Results of Experiments at the Ontario Agricultural College. This is Bulletin No. 228 of the Ontario Department of Agriculture, and prepared by Prof. C. A. Zavitz, Professor of Cereal Husbandry at the Ontario Agricultural College. It deals with experiments made in the raising of each of the regular field crops and of other important crops, chiefly for fodder not now well-known to many of the Ontario farmers. These tests were conducted at the Ontario Agricultural College farm under the direction of the author, who gives, in this bulletin, much valuable advice regarding the possible increase of farm produce, rotation of crops, etc. The author also urges that special attention be given to the raising of

field roots for seed in Ontario, as much of such seed up to the present time has been imported from European countries now at war. The following four very practical rules for producing satisfactory field crops are given:

1. Raise only such crops as are likely to meet the demand.

2. Select good, plump seed which has been tested for vitalit .

3. Give the land early and thorough cultivation.

4. Sow all crops at the proper time and according to right methods.

MANITOBA.

Report of the Department of Agriculture and Immigration for the fiscal year ending November 30, 1914. This volume of 130 pages embodies a record of the accomplishments of the department in its several branches which are treated under the following headings: Agricultural College, Dairying, Horticulture, Noxious Weeds. Protection of Game, Live Stock Associations, Registration of Stallions, Immigration Agricultural Societies, College Extension Work, Home Economic Societies, etc. In his introductory letter to the Minister, the Deputy Minister refers to many successful measures introduced for the first time, much of which he states were made possible owing to the very liberal grant made to the province by the Federal Government in accordance with THE AGRICULTURAL INSTRUCTION ACT.

SASKATCHEWAN

Annual Report of the Saskatchewan Live Stock Associations. This pamphlet gives the annual report for 1914 of the Saskatchewan Horse Breeders' Association, Cattle Breeders' Association, Sheep Breeders' Association, Swine Breeders' Association, and includes the programme for the annual meetings held in March, 1915.

BRITISH COLUMBIA

Protection of Canadian Apples. This is a circular compiled for the British Columbia Fruit Growers' Association and sets forth the present situation of the fruit-growing industry of Canada and in particular that of British Columbia. The memorandum shows, under the following heads, some of the essential conditions affecting the success of Canada's apple industry: (1) Production in the United States; (2) Western Canada as a market for apples; (3) Influence of United States' apples in Canadian markets; (4) Canada's orchard industry; (5) The British Columbia Orchard Industry.

Fire-Blight, (Bacillus Amylovorus—Burrill), Circular No. 23 of the Horticultural Branch of the British Columbia Department of Agriculture, prepared by W. H. Brittain, B.S.A., and B. Hoy, B.S.A. This circular discusses Fire-Blight under the following heads: Cause of Disease, Signs of Disease, How the Disease is Spread, Factors which Influence the Control of Blight, Winter Injury of Blight, Cultural Conditions, Summer Cutting, Distance to Cut, Cutting in the Dormant Season, Methods of Cutting in Winter, Corrosive Sublimate and Susceptibility of Varieties. The circular is also suitably illustrated.

Instruction to Secretaries. This is a circular issued by the Farmers' Institute Branch of the British Columbia Department of Agriculture, and gives instructions in connection with the rules and regulations governing farmers' institutes.

MISCELLANEOUS

A complete report of the *Potato Growing Contest for Boys in Carleton and Russell Counties* during the years 1913 and 1914 has recently been issued by the committee in charge, consisting of Mr. R. B. Whyte, Ottawa, Mr. L. H. Newman, B. S. A., Secretary Canadian Seed Growers' Association, Ottawa, Mr. W. D. Jackson, B. S. A., Agricultural Representative for Carleton County, Carp, Ont., and Mr. W. T. Macoun, Dominion Horticulturist, Ottawa.

This report includes the organization and rules of the contest, results of the contests in Carleton County in 1913 and 1914, and results of the Russell County contests in 1913 and 1914, with a complete report of the public meetings held in both years,

also a summary of the results obtained in these contests.

Lethbridge Board of Trade Annual Report, 1914. This report gives the population of Lethbridge as 10,147, and the school enrolment as 1,888. The Board has a membership of 219. The president is G. R. Marnoch. It is stated that the activities of the Board have been mainly applied to the furtherance of agriculture, and its allied industries. Considerable attention has been paid with gratifying success to irrigation. With a view to helping farmers to acquire suitable live stock, sixty citizens pledged themselves to the extent of $150 each. The nine thousand dollars thus raised was loaned at five per cent to farmers, who with their notes also gave a lien on their cattle, repayment being spread over two years. Farmers, backed by the Board of Trade, have petitioned the Federal Government to extend its irrigation work. Efforts are also being made to develop the well water supplies. The Rural Relations Committee of the Board are taking an active part in furthering these matters and promoting the "back to the land" movement. The Board advocates the establishment of Demonstration Farms.

The Provincial Government is urged to take steps to institute a farmers' page in every daily and weekly paper in the province. Other practical subjects are referred to such as the progress of dry farming, sugar beet cultivation, etc. Satisfactory advancement is reported in live stock breeding and butter-making.

NOTES

The Ontario Agricultural Experimental Union has announced that some 30 experiments with grain, fodder crops, roots, grasses, clover and alfalfas will be conducted throughout the province of Ontario during the year 1915.

Plans are being formed to settle a few of Regina's outlaying sub-divisions with market gardeners. A company has been formed, under the name of the Regina Garden City and Agricultural Company, which will break two or three hundred acres of land just north of the city and rent it out in five-acre plots to Belgian refugees for market garden purposes. The company is stated to have already got into touch with nearly a hundred Belgians in Holland, France and England, and it is expected by the Regina men that a large number will be brought over later on in the summer when the situation opens up.

During the year 1914, the Department of Agriculture of British Columbia conducted a number of Women's Institute competitions. These were for Institutes having the best average attendance based on membership, for Institutes having the best programme for 1914, and for the best papers by Institute members on specified subjects.

The Provincial Apiarist at the Ontario Agricultural College, Mr. Morley Pettit, has issued a circular warning bee-keepers to be careful to prevent robbing during the warm days of spring and directing attention to the clause of the law prohibiting the use of immovable frame hives. With the circular he forwards a review of the season of 1914 which he describes as one of the poorest for honey production ever known.

With a view to further the efforts of the Department of Agriculture to arouse a widespread interest in corn growing on the part of Western farmers, a number of the leading banks in Saskatchewan have joined in an arrangement under which, in every district where any stock raising prevails, selected seed will be supplied free to a limited number of farmers who will undertake to grow an acre of corn or green fodder in accordance with instructions furnished by the Department of Agriculture. The action of the banks in this case has been taken with the cordial support of the Department of Agriculture.

The city of Lethbridge is taking up the question of having unused areas of land within the city made available for the growing of garden crops. Unfinished boulevards along the streets are being assigned to citizens who will agree to use them for gardening purposes. Mr. A. M. Grace, Commissioner of Public Works for the city, advises that quite a number have already been granted allotments and applications are still being received. Victoria Park, comprising ten acres, has been let to one grower who will probably devote it to the growing of potatoes. Henderson Park, consisting of thirty-five acres, will be devoted to the growing of oats for the city.

The Charlottetown Guardian of March 4th contains the article by R. H. Campbell, Superintendent of Education, on Elementary Agricultural Instruction that appeared in the February number of the AGRICULTURAL GAZETTE. It also contained the following editorial:

"The article, elsewhere in this issue, on Instruction in Elementary Agriculture, by Mr. R. H. Campbell, Superintendent of Education, will, we feel sure, be read with pleasure and profit. Prince Edward Island has won a name for itself in the fact that it is the first of the Canadian provinces to successfully solve the hitherto difficult problem of co-ordinating agricultural and primary school education. Heretofore the agricultural and educational departments carried out their respective activities, each under its own management and with little regard for the inter-relation. As a result there was overlapping and duplication and agricultural education, although attempted, was unsatisfactory and unpractical. As a result of the policy adopted by Premier Mathieson a common basis has been found, and agricultural instruction now goes hand in hand with the ordinary routine work of the schools. As explained by Superintendent Campbell, the schools are under the direct supervision of inspectors, who are not only educationists, but practical agriculturists. This is as it should be, especially in a province like ours, whose basic industry is agriculture."

Advices received from different parts of the country confirm the good impression conveyed by the reports of the recently held conferences. Dealing with the province of Ontario, in the counties of Peel, Lambton, Durham, Simcoe, Middlesex, Oxford, Brant, Wentworth and Waterloo, an increase of fall wheat sown is reported of from 25 to 30 per cent. From Manitoulin Island and the Districts of Kenora, Temiscaming and Rainy River the stories are the same, as promising abundant crops with a favourable season. In Lambton an increased growth of vegetables is expected and in Norfolk hopes are entertained for good oats, barley, corn, bean and apple crops, but of potatoes there is a decrease in cultivation owing to the prices that prevailed in the district this year. In Dundas more land is said to have been broken and an increase of 10 per cent in spring wheat is anticipated. A decrease, however, in dairy products is thought likely owing to disposal of stock by the farmers. From Peel something of the same kind is reported.

Three propositions have been put up to the farmers of Canada in the "Patriotism and Production" campaign:—

1. Grow staple crops, such as can be stored and transported. There will be a special demand for wheat, oats, peas, beans and flax.

2. Increase production per acre rather than increase acreage. Better cultivation and the best seed will double or treble the yield under favourable weather conditions.

3. Particular attention should be given to live stock. The war put up the price of cereals more than the price of meats—but there is coming a world shortage of meats. It was in sight before the war. Out of the great cattle countries in only one have the cattle kept pace with the people.

The Department of Education of Saskatchewan has recently appointed Miss Fannie A. Twiss of Galt, Ont., Director of Household Science for the province. In connection with the instruction in Agriculture, an Agricultural Instruction Committee has also been appointed to advise on all matter pertaining to the scope and character of agricultural education in the public, high and normal schools. This committee consists of D. P. McColl, Superintendent of Education; W. J. Rutherford, Dean of College of Agriculture, Saskatoon; J. A. Snell, Principal of Normal School, Saskatoon; Dr. R. A. Wilson, Principal of Normal School, Regina; A. F. Mantle, Deputy Minister of Agriculture, and A. H. Ball, Deputy Minister of Education.

INDEX TO PERIODICAL LITERATURE.

One Great Accomplishment on Corn Breeding. The Story of "Reid's Yellow Dent" as told by Miss Olive G. Reid, a daughter of the originator of the type, *Breeders Gazette*, Chicago, February 25, 1915, page 383.

The Facts About Corn Growing in Minnesota, Applying Scientific Principles to Actual Practice in the Corn Field.— Preparation of the Seed-bed, Planting the Seed, Cultivation—Improving the Yield and Quality by Proper Selection and Handling of the Seed, by R. D. Smith, Mgr., Homewood Farm, Swift Co., Minn., *The Farmer*, St. Paul, Minn., February 27, 1915, page 339.

The Story of Corn Improvement in Minnesota. Breeding and Cultural Methods followed by Expert Corn Growers to Obtain Results in Quality and Yield— Prominent winners at Minnesota Corn Show tell the readers of *The Farmer* the Reasons for Their Success, *The Farmer*, St. Paul, Minn., February 27, 1915, page 341.

There's Money in Getting Together. Associations in the West handle Fencing, Flour, Timber, Seed Grain and other Farm Supplies. Prosperity follows. By W. W. Thomson, *Farmer's Magazine*, Toronto, March 1, 1915, page 21.

Give $1,000—Don't Consolidate, by E. C. Drury, *Farmer's Magazine*, Toronto. March 1, 1915, page 7.

Eating Money from Sandhills, by L. Stevenson, *Farmer's Magazine*, Toronto, March 1, 1915, page 17.

Cool-Headed View on "Patriotism and Production", *The North West Farmer*, Winnipeg, March 5, 1915, page 194.

School Gardening, by H. W. Watson, Provincial Superintendent of Elementary Agriculture for Manitoba. *The Grain Growers' Guide*, Winnipeg, March 3, 1915, page 8.

The Soil and the Seed, by Seager Wheeler, Rosthern, Sask., *The Grain Growers' Guide*, Winnipeg, Man., March 3, 1915, page 11.

Gardening in Rural Schools, by E. Leroy Churchill, *Farm and Ranch Review*, Calgary, March 5, 1915, page 150.

Lost—Ten Million Dollars a Day. An Interview with the Assistant Secretary of Agriculture, by William Harper Dean, *The Saturday Evening Post*, Philadelphia, Pa., March 15, 1915, page 25.

Problems of the Minnesota Potato Industry. Methods of Minnesota growers observed by the world's leading potato expert. Possibilities of the crop in this state not yet reached. Seed selection, better culture and control of disease essential to success. *The Farmer*, St. Paul, Minn., March 20, 1915.

The Wisconsin Potato Growers' Association. Development work in Wisconsin which is leading toward standardization of varieties, disease control and standard market grades. An address before the newly organized potato growers of Minnesota, by J. W. Hicks, President, Wisconsin Potato Growers' Association. *The Farmer*, St. Paul, Minn., March 20, 1915.

Alfalfa Production, by F. S. Grisdale, B. S. A., Agronomist, School of Agriculture, Olds, Alberta, *Farmer's Advocate*, Winnipeg, March 4, 1915.

The Forthcoming Situation in Agricultural Work,

Prof. L. H. Bailey, Vice-President and Chairman of Section L. American Association for the Advancement of Science, *Science*, February 26th, 1915.

A Big Bank Engages a Professor,

The Banker Farmer, Champaign, Ill., April, 1915, page 2. Prof. H. R. Smith, formerly of the Minnesota College of Agriculture, treats of what he expects to accomplish.

The Poultry Short Course at Guelph,

The Canadian Poultry Review, Toronto, April, 1914, page 147.

Wheat Breeding. Many Genetists Working with Important Cereal Crop—What they have Accomplished—Hope for Future Improvement—Methods of Procedure,

A. E. V. Richardson, Agricultural Superintendent, Victoria Department of Agriculture, Melbourne, Australia, *Journal of Heredity*, Washington, D.C., March, 1915.

School Gardening,

H. W. Watson, Provincial Superintendent of Elementary Agriculture for Manitoba, *The Grain Growers' Guide*, Winnipeg, March 3rd, 1915, page 8.

CPSIA information can be obtained
at www.ICGtesting.com
Printed in the USA
BVHW041000030119
536964BV00004B/23/P